# A HALF CENTURY

*of*

# UNION

# THEOLOGICAL

# SEMINARY

*1896–1945*

*AN INFORMAL HISTORY*

*by*

HENRY SLOANE COFFIN

CHARLES SCRIBNER'S SONS

*New York  1954*

# CONTENTS

# A HALF CENTURY
# OF UNION THEOLOGICAL SEMINARY

# FOREWORD

THE history of the first sixty years of Union Theological Seminary (1836–1896) had been recorded in two large volumes by the late Professor George L. Prentiss.[1] But, up to this time, there has been no printed account of the past half century. Accordingly, the Directors of the Seminary asked President-emeritus Henry Sloane Coffin to bring Dr. Prentiss' chronicle down to the present.

It is hardly necessary to stress Dr. Coffin's ideal equipment for this task. He had entered Union Seminary as a student just at the turn of the century, in the autumn of 1899. But his father, Edmund Coffin, had been advisor to several of the Seminary directors for many years previous, including not a few marked by stress and conflict. It was in a home where the affairs of Union Seminary were a constant and major concern that Henry Coffin had grown up. Thus, he was well acquainted with the Seminary's background and much of its earlier history.

Dr. Coffin's direct association with the Seminary exactly spans the half century here surveyed—first, as a student and resident graduate; then, from 1904 to 1926, as Assistant and Associate Professor of Homiletics and Pastoral Theology; then, from 1926 to 1945, as President of the Faculty.

Dr. Coffin was encouraged to draw heavily upon his own

---

[1]*Fifty Years of the Union Theological Seminary*, published in 1889, and *Another Decade in the History of the Union Theological Seminary*, 1899.

1

unique familiarity with the Seminary's affairs. This suggestion proved congenial to him. The result is almost a "personal
history," an account of Union Seminary's life and problems
through the first half of the twentieth century as they appeared to the man who had a larger influence upon them,
as well as a more intimate knowledge of them, than any other
person. As such it is certain to hold special interest for the
Seminary alumni.

No admonition was more frequently impressed by Dr.
Coffin upon his faculty colleagues, alumni and students than
this: "Union Seminary lives by its brains." By this he meant
that, since almost alone among theological schools in the
United States, this Seminary enjoys no official ecclesiastical
or university sponsorship, it must depend for its ability to
attract able students and to exert influence in American
Church life upon the scholarly eminence and teaching skill
of its professors. To Dr. Coffin, Union Seminary has been
largely the men who have composed its Faculty. And so, his
account follows Dr. Prentiss' earlier histories by focussing
upon biographical sketches and appraisals of individual teachers, for which he has claimed the collaboration of a large
number of their abler students. With one or two exceptions,
these biographies have been confined to Professors who have
completed their active service on the Faculty.

Obviously, it would have been inappropriate, as well as
impossible, for Dr. Coffin to give a just appraisal of his own
administration of the Presidency, which occupied almost half
of the period under review. Dr. Morgan P. Noyes, whose close
association with Dr. Coffin as well as with the Seminary, as
student, Instructor, Director and Associate Professor, covers
more than forty years, has been asked to fill in what other-

wise would be a large and inexcusable lacuna in the record. A brief "Afterword" summarises some of the major changes in the life and work of the Seminary since Dr. Coffin's retirement from the Presidency up to the date of publication.

Professor-emeritus Harold H. Tryon who served at Dr. Coffin's right hand throughout his Presidency, and Professor Cyril C. Richardson as the Seminary's official archivist, have assisted with the details of the manuscript.

The Seminary is deeply indebted to Dr. Coffin for his characteristic readiness to undertake this task which, while it has doubtless been a "labor of love," has made heavy and irksome demands upon his time and strength.

HENRY P. VAN DUSEN,
President.

Union Theological Seminary,

January 1, 1954

# CHAPTER I

# UNION THEOLOGICAL SEMINARY
# IN THE NINETEENTH CENTURY

On the tenth day of October 1835, a group of nine men assembled in the home of Knowles Taylor, at 8 Bond St. New York City, to consider whether the time had come for the establishment of another theological seminary. When the question had been decided affirmatively, the group added to their number, and were twenty-eight at the time they applied for a charter in 1836. They continued to meet at Mr. Taylor's home. A half century later, his daughter recalled that as a little girl she saw the chairs in the parlor arranged for these meetings. They were all Presbyterians, ministers or elders, but "ecumenical" Presbyterians, foremost in interdenominational organizations and eager for the co-operation of all Christians in the work of the kingdom of God. The ministers were pastors of city congregations or executives of missionary organizations; the laymen were merchants and lawyers conspicuous for their integrity and Christian zeal. They were practical men who had been warmed by the revival of religion which had been in progress in 1829–32. Their primary concern was for the Christianization of our rapidly growing nation and for the evangelization of the non-Christian peoples of mankind. Before their eyes, as they put it, were "the claims of the world upon the Church of Christ."

These were the major motives which prompted them to launch a new theological seminary and to locate it in New York City. But two other considerations weighed strongly in their minds. On the one hand, current controversies which divided Christians into hostile camps grieved their souls, for they distracted attention from the main business of the Church, as these men saw it. On the other hand, as residents of "the greatest and most growing community in America," they were keenly alive to the special problems of churches in urban centers and of the inadequacy of existing seminaries in preparing men for their leadership. They believed that "large cities furnish many peculiar facilities and advantages" for ministerial training.

The controversies of the time were in the main in two areas:

(1) There were doctrinal conflicts over fine points in theology, which to the founders of Union Seminary had no relevance to Christian life and work. They resented heresy-hunting which prompted attacks upon ministers to whom they looked up as honored leaders of the Church. In that very month of October 1835, a well-known pastor, and one whom they knew and revered, was being charged with heresy before the Presbytery of Philadelphia. Here were the charges brought against the Rev. Albert Barnes:

1. Mr. Barnes teaches that "all sin consists in voluntary action."
2. He teaches "that Adam (before and after his fall) was ignorant of his moral relations to such a degree that he did not know the consequences of his sin would or should reach any further than to natural death."
3. He teaches that "unregenerate men are able to keep the commandments and convert themselves to God."

4. He asserts that "faith is an act of the mind, and not a principle, and is itself imputed for righteousness."

5. He denies "that God entered into covenant with Adam constituting him a federal or covenant head, and representative to all his natural descendants."

6. He denies "that the first sin of Adam is imputed to all his posterity."

7. He denies "that mankind are guilty, i.e., liable to punishment on account of the sin of Adam."

8. He denies "that Christ suffered the proper penalty of the law as the vicarious substitute of his people, and thus took away legally their sins and purchased pardon."

9. He denies "that the righteousness, i.e., the active obedience of Christ to the law, is imputed to his people for their justification; so that they are righteous in the eye of the law, and therefore justified."

10. He also teaches, "in opposition to the Standards, that justification is simply pardon."

The leaders of the theological seminary of the Church, located at Princeton, were aligned against Mr. Barnes, and to these New York Presbyterians their attitude seemed intolerant. In 1840 they elected Mr. Barnes a director of their Seminary and he served for thirty years until his death in 1870. He delivered the first course of lectures on the Ely Foundation in 1867 upon "The Evidences of Christianity in the Nineteenth Century."

In New England, Lyman Beecher had been assailed. They admired him for his championship of evangelical religion against Unitarianism, for his courageous opposition to intemperance in drink and to duelling, and perhaps even more for the patriotism which had led him on the verge of old age to leave a prominent Boston pulpit and throw in his lot with the Christian forces in "the great valley of the West" at Cincinnati. Why a man of such missionary passion with such a record of service should be condemned for minor deviations from conventional orthodoxy passed their comprehension.

Nearer home, this assault launched against Albert Barnes, whose *Notes on the New Testament* was read in their homes, and who was himself the trusted personal friend of many of them, roused their indignation, and was the proximate cause of their meeting to consider a new theological seminary. How could a man so peaceable, so devoted to the Bible, so indefatigable in his work, rising at 4:00 A.M. to secure uninterrupted quiet for his Bible study which had produced the prized *Notes,* and to conserve a full normal day for his pastoral labors, be accused of heresy? And how remote from practical Christian life the ten charges were! At the very time of their first meeting his synod had forbidden his preaching and his pulpit was being supplied by other ministers. These charges against Albert Barnes were to their practical minds "extremes of doctrinal speculation."

While later generations smile at the minutiae of doctrine over which Presbyterians fought so seriously, we must recall that other communions in that epoch had their internal conflicts. The Protestant Episcopal Church felt the impact of the Tractarian Movement in the Church of England and found High Churchman and Evangelical pitted against each other. Two of its bishops were also in difficulties. In Philadelphia, the bishop was suspended from his episcopal office for excessive drinking and his brother, bishop of New York, in the same year was presented for "licentiousness," and similarly suspended.

For weal or for woe Union Theological Seminary was bound up with the tradition of Presbyterianism and has been involved in its strifes in the realm of doctrine. Intellectual competency, rather than ritualistic or doctrinal conformity, was to be exacted of its professors.

(2) Again there was heated argument over the institution of slavery. None of the founders of the Seminary favored its continuance, and some were fervent in seeking its end. But they viewed some contemporary abolitionists as fanatics, whose extreme statements and actions were jeopardizing the unity of the nation. They wished slavery done away by peaceful and legal means, with due compensation to the owners for the property rights involved. On the current scene in politics Daniel Webster represented their views.

Heretofore, schools of divinity in this country had been located in small towns where in the quiet of rural surroundings professors and students could pursue their labors without interruption. But the movement towards the growth of cities was in full swing, and these men felt that the years to come would call for many ministers of urban congregations who could cope with the problems of folk in crowded areas. They saw practical advantages for students who would find in cities readier means of self-support while they studied; and who would face urban problems in the congregations where they worshipped and worked.

They further hoped to enlist among the young men of New York and Brooklyn recruits for the ministry. While the rest of their program was justified in years to come, this last hope has never been fulfilled; the majority of the students have come from all over the country and from other lands, and the neighboring cities of New York and Brooklyn have furnished only a small minority of the total. But the great city has exercised a drawing pull upon young people, and contributed in no small degree to the numbers who sought this seminary as the training school for their ministry.

To these earnest and devout men, the hour had come for the establishment of a new theological seminary,

around which all men of moderate views and feelings, who desire to live free from party strife, and to stand aloof from all extremes of doctrinal speculation, practical radicalism and ecclesiastical domination, may cordially and affectionately rally.

At the first meeting Knowles Taylor was placed in the chair and the Rev. Erskine Mason made secretary, and it was resolved

that it is expedient, depending on the blessing of God, to establish a theological seminary in this city.

## DESIGN OF THE FOUNDERS

The founders had a clear conception of the kind of seminary they had in mind. In the Preamble to the Constitution, adopted by them on January 18, 1836, they specified three requisites uppermost in their thought for would-be ministers:

(1) "A full and thorough education." We have spoken of them as practical men, merchants and pastors of city congregations but they laid stress on "solid learning." As an example of their lofty and exigent academic standards we may cite the scholar whom they chose for the Chair of Biblical Literature. Dr. Edward Robinson was an eminent Orientalist and an archeologist whose name is still associated with an

arch which he discovered in Jerusalem, and which fixes the level of the streets about the temple in the days of Christ. In his letter accepting the appointment Dr. Robinson wrote:

To understand the Bible, the student must know all about the Bible. It is not a mere smattering of Greek and Hebrew, not the mere ability to consult a text in the original Scriptures, that can qualify him to be an interpreter of the word of life. He must be thoroughly furnished for his work, if he be expected to do his work well. A bare enumeration of the particulars that fall within the department of Biblical Literature will show that it covers a wider field than is generally supposed. To it, properly, belong full courses of instruction in the Hebrew, Greek and Chaldee languages, and also, as auxiliaries, in the Syriac, Arabic, and other minor dialects; in Biblical Introduction or the History of the Bible as a whole, and its various parts, its writers, its manuscripts, editions, etc.; in Biblical Criticism or the history and condition of the text; in Biblical Hermeneutics, or the theory and principles of Interpretation; in Biblical Exegesis, or the practical application of those principles to the study and interpretation of the sacred books; in Biblical Antiquities; and, further, a separate consideration of the version of the Seventy [i.e., the "Septuagint"], as a chief source of illustration for both the Old and New Testaments.

This letter penned to men just starting a new enterprise and beset with most pressing financial difficulties shows the calibre of the scholarship they were enlisting and the large views for the future development of the course of instruction which its first professors entertained.

## PREAMBLE TO THE CONSTITUTION

### Adopted January 18, 1836

That the design of the founders of this institution may be fully known to all whom it may concern, and be sacredly regarded by the directors, professors, and students, it is judged proper to make the following preliminary statement:

1. A number of Christians, clergymen and laymen, in the cities of New York and Brooklyn, deeply impressed with the claims of the world upon the church of Christ to furnish a competent supply of well-educated and pious ministers of correct principles, to preach the Gospel to every creature; impressed also with the inadequacy of all existing means for this purpose; and believing that large cities furnish many peculiar facilities and advantages for conducting theological education; after several meetings for consultation and prayer:

RESOLVED, unanimously, in humble dependence on the grace of God, to attempt the establishment of a Theological Seminary in the City of New York.

2. The institution (while it will receive others to the advantages it may furnish) is principally designed for such young men in the cities of New York and Brooklyn as are, or may be, desirous of pursuing a course of theological study, and whose circumstances render it inconvenient for them to go from home for this purpose.

3. It is the design of the founders to furnish the means of a full and thorough education, in all the subjects taught in the best theological seminaries in the United States, and also to embrace therewith a thorough knowledge of the standards of faith and discipline of the Presbyterian Church.

4. Being fully persuaded that vital godliness well proved, a thorough education and a wholesome practical training in works

of benevolence and pastoral labors are all essentially necessary to meet the wants and promote the best interests of the Kingdom of Christ, the founders of this Seminary design that its students, living and acting under pastoral influence, and performing the important duties of church members in the several churches to which they belong, or with which they worship, in prayer meetings, in the instruction of Sabbath schools and Bible classes, and being conversant with all the social benevolent efforts of this important location, shall have the opportunity of adding to solid learning and true piety, enlightened experience.

5. By the foregoing advantages, the founders hope and expect, with the blessing of God, to call forth from these two flourishing cities, and to enlist in the service of Christ and in the work of the ministry, genius, talent, enlightened piety, and missionary zeal; and to qualify many for the labors and management of the various religious institutions, seminaries of learning, and enterprises of benevolence, which characterize the present times.

6. Finally, it is the design of the founders to provide a theological seminary in the midst of the greatest and most growing community in America, around which all men of moderate views and feelings, who desire to live free from party strife, and to stand aloof from all the extremes of doctrinal speculation, practical radicalism, and ecclesiastical domination, may cordially and affectionately rally.

### Requirements of the Charter

The charter provides that "equal privileges of admission and instruction, with all the advantages of the Institution, shall be allowed to students of every denomination of Christians."

(2) "Vital godliness well proved." They had no question that God's Spirit alone can call and equip a minister of the Gospel. The testing of a student's vital godliness is beyond human power, but they wished a seminary where such vital godliness would flourish and warm and empower the "solid learning" they were so sedulously seeking to provide. Their success from the start to this hour is attested by the numbers from the Seminary who have enlisted for service on mission fields, and by the spiritual quality of the vast majority of the Seminary's alumni. The religious life within the institution has always been a major concern both of Directors and Faculty, and also of the leaders of the student body.

(3) "A wholesome practical training in works of benevolence and pastoral labors." This was one of the advantages which they foresaw in locating the Seminary "in the midst of the greatest and most growing community in America." They wished their students to add "to solid learning and true piety, enlightened experience." From its first year to the present it has insisted that students shall be safeguarded from an "ivory tower" outlook upon the personal and social problems of their day by constant first-hand touch with churches and other institutions grappling with them, and shall have part in the evangelistic and educational work of congregations.

The prescience of the founders was extraordinary. Dr. Prentiss at the Seminary's fiftieth anniversary dwelt on the accuracy of their foresight, and now, more than one hundred and fifteen years from the foundation, we gauge how closely the Union Seminary of today corresponds with the main outlines of the design which they drew. It is a tradition that Dr. Erskine Mason was the writer of the Preamble—a noble document both in language and in its ideas, and one which has played a decisive role in the life of the institution throughout its history.

A noteworthy instance of the fidelity of the Seminary to the inclusiveness of this Preamble occurred in connection with the election of its first Professor of Church History in 1850. The Board invited to this Chair Henry Boynton Smith who had taught at Andover Theological Seminary and at Amherst College. He had studied in Germany and was an exponent of the historical method in the investigation of the Bible and of the doctrines of the Church, an admirer of Schleiermacher. His friends warned him against leaving New England, and coming under the tyranny of what he himself termed "the consistent domineering Presbyterianism." However, he had convinced himself that the ecclesiastical principles of the Presbyterianism of the New School Church and of the old Congregationalism of New England were essentially the same, and he arrived in New York and discussed the theological basis of the Seminary frankly with its leaders. In a letter written at the time he reported:

Last evening I spent wholly, till eleven o'clock and after, with Dr. White, talking over the whole Seminary and matters thereto belonging. He was rather curious about some of my theological opinions, and we got into a regular discussion of two hours on the person of Christ, in which he claimed that I advocated something inconsistent with the Catechism, and I claimed that he taught what was against the Catechism, which was rather a hard saying against an old-established professor of theology. However, it was all very well and kind on both sides, and did not prevent his urging my coming here.

Enough has been said to make plain the design of the

founders. They deliberately did not place their institution under the control of any ecclesiastical body. They were impatient of the interruption of the preaching of so useful a minister as Albert Barnes, and they sought a charter from the legislature of the State of New York which vested the final government of the Seminary in its own Board of Directors. They have been spoken of as "ecumenical" Presbyterians, and while that word was not in general use in the 1830's, it is justified by a clause which they inserted in the Charter:

Equal privileges of admission and instruction, with all the advantages of the Institution, shall be allowed to students of every denomination of Christians.

When the rupture of the Presbyterian Church which the founders so much dreaded, came to pass in 1837–38 the overwhelming majority of Directors and Professors joined the New School Church; but it is significant that the minister whom they elected to the Chair of Systematic Theology, Henry White, was in and remained with the Old School Church. The liberality of liberals is commonly extended to those who share their position or are more radical than they, but often does not extend to their more conservative opponents. These practical men of "moderate views" strove to continue inclusive in their sympathies, true Catholics in the original sense of that sorely abused word.

## RELATIONS WITH THE PRESBYTERIAN CHURCH[1]

The controversies of the 1830's died down, and after the War between the States, the late 1860's saw attempts made

---

[1] It is not the purpose of this book to record the history of the Seminary through its first half century. That has been done with skill and accuracy by

to heal the breach in the Presbyterian Church. Among the reconcilers, none were more prominent than members of Union's Board of Directors and Faculty. Its then President of the Board, Dr. William Adams, was made Chairman of the New School Committee which negotiated the terms of re-union. In that connection he was appealed to by the authorities of Princeton Theological Seminary to obtain relief for them from a system of electing their professors which was becoming intolerable. The professors were chosen by the General Assembly, but so large a body could not know the qualifications of a scholar nor become familiar with his aptness to teach. Accordingly, it was proposed that the Boards of Directors in the various seminaries of the reunited Church should be given the power to elect the professors, but it was stipulated that their names should be reported to the General Assembly and that should the Assembly disapprove the election, it was null and void. The memorial to the Assembly in this matter was prepared by Dr. William Adams, and brought to the Union Seminary Board of Directors; but one of them, D. Willis James, opposed its passage as "a very serious mistake, and calculated to produce great and unfortunate mischief." The tide of feeling for reunion was running strong, and Dr. Adams was eager to promote peace and harmony in the reunited Church. The Memorial in its essential sentences read:

That the General Assembly may be pleased to adopt it as a

---

the late Professor George L. Prentiss in his volume, *Fifty Years of the Union Theological Seminary,* published in 1889. Nor is it the purpose of this book to go into the details of the heresy trial of Professor Charles Augustus Briggs. These have been fully dealt with in a second volume by Professor Prentiss, *Another Decade in the History of the Union Theological Seminary,* 1899. The present writer graduated in the Class of 1900, and has been asked to cover primarily the five decades with which he is personally familiar.

rule and plan, in the exercise of the proprietorship and control over the several theological seminaries, that so far as the election of professors is concerned the Assembly will commit the same to their respective Boards of Directors, on the following terms and conditions:

1. That the Board of Directors of each theological seminary shall be authorized to appoint all professors of the same.

2. That all such appointments shall be reported to the General Assembly, and no such appointment shall be considered a complete election if disapproved by a majority vote of the Assembly.

This Memorial was adopted by the General Assembly of 1870; and Union Seminary, which heretofore had been completely autonomous, accepted it as an agreement between the Seminary and the General Assembly of the Presbyterian Church.

No action was taken under this agreement until twenty-one years later when the transfer of Professor Charles A. Briggs from the Chair of Hebrew to that of Biblical Theology was reported to the Assembly of 1891. Dr. Briggs was not being appointed a professor for the first time: he had served for seventeen years. Nor was this a new election, but a transfer from one chair to another. The Directors were unaware that it could be disapproved, for it did not strictly come under the terms of the agreement. But alarm that the authority of the Bible was menaced by historical study was running high throughout the Church, and Dr. Briggs by his writings and especially by his inaugural address on entering upon the new chair had fanned the flames. The General Assembly voted its disapproval of the transfer, and appointed a committee to confer with the Directors.

To see the attacks upon Professor Briggs in perspective,

it must be recalled that it was not Presbyterians only who in the closing years of the nineteenth and the opening years of the twentieth centuries found themselves involved in heresy trials. The Congregationalists, most forward to glory in their liberties, had the serious Andover controversy in the 1880's over what was called "second probation," and later dropped Professor George H. Gilbert from the Faculty of their Chicago Theological Seminary. The Methodist bishops refused to sanction the reappointment of Professor Hinckley G. Mitchell to his Chair at Boston University. The Episcopalians deposed from the ministry the Rev. Algernon S. Crapsey for questioning the historic basis of the Virgin Birth of Christ. The Roman Catholics imposed an anti-modernist oath, and removed outstanding scholars who were pursuing investigations into historic origins. Fear of heresy was in the air and legal methods of maintaining sound doctrine were resorted to on both sides of the Atlantic and in many communions.

It is not part of the design of this book to trace the course of the controversy over Professor Briggs, which ended in his being placed on trial for heresy before the Presbytery of New York, where he was acquitted. His opponents, however, appealed to the General Assembly, passing over the Synod of New York, the next tribunal in the Presbyterian system (for they knew it was likely to follow the Presbytery's verdict), and the Assembly took the case, declared him guilty and suspended him from the ministry. One may comment, these more than sixty years later, that the main "heresies" for which he was condemned are today taught in many of the most orthodox seminaries in this country and in practically all of those under the immediate jurisdiction of the Presbyterian Church.

The Board of Directors promptly sought legal advice to make sure where the Seminary then stood. They were told that their action of May 1870, in which they had voluntarily surrendered some of their power in the appointment of professors, had been *extra vires*. Under their Charter they could not divest themselves or share with another body any of their responsibility for the governance of the Seminary. They had been unfaithful to the intention of the founders in submitting in any degree to "ecclesiastical domination." They accordingly rescinded their Memorial to the General Assembly of 1870 and resumed their former independence. They retained Professor Briggs in his chair and expressed their confidence in him. There were threatenings from various quarters that suits would be instituted to recover from them funds declared the property of the Presbyterian Church, but no such suits were begun, because would-be litigants were told by lawyers that, in the light of the Seminary's Charter, they had no legal grounds. Further it was well known that the principal donors to the Seminary and their heirs were fully aware of the Seminary's independence and heartily approved of it.

# CHAPTER II

## THE PRESIDENCY OF
## CHARLES CUTHBERT HALL, 1897–1908

In 1897 the last survivor of those who had founded the Seminary, the eminent lawyer, Charles Butler, LL.D., President of the Board of Directors, passed away at the age of ninety-five. He had succeeded Richard T. Haines in that office in 1870 and had been a leader of the Seminary during quiet and most stormy years. The Board chose John Crosby Brown to fill his office; and that same year (1897) elected one of their own number, Charles Cuthbert Hall, both Professor of Pastoral Theology, Church Polity and Missions, and President of the Faculty. For twenty years Dr. Hall had been pastor of the First Presbyterian Church of Brooklyn and counsellor in spiritual things to numbers outside his own congregation.

No happier choice could have been made. Dr. Thomas S. Hastings, tall and commanding in figure, precise in habit and in speech, had led the Seminary through years of strife with courage, resoluteness and tact. Dr. Hall had an outgoing nature and made almost everyone he met feel his personal interest in him. Someone wrote, "He never gave the impression that he was looking over your shoulder at the next person to be interviewed." He was a convinced believer in liberty in research and teaching, and a man of vision and untiring energy. Dr. Hall was a mystic who adored his Saviour. A characteristic address to his students was from the text: "And when I saw Him, I fell at His feet as dead." He warmed the Seminary from his entrance on his office until his sorely regretted death in 1908.

In his inaugural address President Hall sketched his vision of the Seminary's advance in the immediate future along four lines: (1) academic; (2) University extension; (3) social service; (4) spiritual power.

Under the second heading, Dr. Hall spoke of the Seminary as embarking on a program for training lay workers. Nothing was done immediately to implement this program. But in 1901 two men were appointed for this extension work. The first was the Rev. Richard Morse Hodge, a graduate of Princeton College and Seminary, who was serving at Nashville, Tennessee, as superintendent of the Biblical Institute for Christian Workers. Dr. Hodge was a man of intellectual ability and devout spirit, but without tact. He was reacting from a very conservative theological position and was belligerently modernist. This was unfortunate in one who was attempting to interpret the Bible to layfolk. On one occasion he was insisting on the ever-changing and progressive quality in Christian minds, and remarked, "Two weeks from now you will hear different views from me." To which a Scots-born elder asked him: "Dr. Hodge, the next time you speak to us, would you kindly give us what you would be willing to stand by for at least a fortnight?" Dr. Hodge became a lecturer on Biblical Literature at Teachers College in 1902. His connection with the Seminary lasted until 1907, and thereafter he went on in Teachers College and in the extension work of Columbia University until 1919.

In 1901 the Seminary also appointed William Dana Street, of the Class of 1898, and Assistant Pastor of the Madison Avenue Reformed Church, Instructor in the English Bible for Lay Workers, a post he held for two years, when he withdrew to give his whole time to a pastorate. The extension program for lay workers had not been carefully thought through and was never very successful. Had Dr. Hall lived and remained in this country, it might possibly have been developed.

Under the third point in his inaugural, Dr. Hall outlined the needs of the upper East Side, and spoke of the Union Settlement founded by men intimately related to Union Seminary and already in operation in a small way. Dr. Hall envisaged a great institutional church where students would work and obtain practical experience. However, the population of the neighborhood where the Settlement was located underwent rapid and radical changes which made it difficult, if not impossible, to carry on a Protestant Church.[2] But Union Settlement has had a splendid history for more than sixty years, and it owed to President Hall the coming of its most potent figure—the Rev. Gaylord S. White, Headworker from 1901 to 1923.

Dr. Hall was pre-eminently a pastor. Students at once became aware of his personal interest in them and his sympathy with their situations. His love of worship was contagious and changed the climate of the Seminary. He had edited a hymnal, played on the piano, and was an enthusiast for reverent music. He captured the hearts of students. He

---

[2]However, in 1948, the Church of the Son of Man next door to Union Settlement, was reopened as a church in connection with the East Harlem Protestant Parish, a new and original attempt to carry the Gospel to the polyglot populace of New York's Upper East Side, and is flourishing under those auspices today.

wrote long letters in his own inimitable hand to entrants and became at once their intimate friend at the Seminary. If he had a fault, it was his inability to assess a man objectively. All his geese were swans. He could not bring himself to believe that any student was not what he should be, and he permitted some to go on into the ministry who should have been weeded out as unfit. Few men on the Faculty have been held in such warm affection. This was as true of employees in the Seminary as of students. His death came as a profound personal loss.

As he went about the country during the all-too-brief years of his presidency, Dr. Hall was an inestimable factor in allaying apprehensions and correcting prejudices, which were the deplorable sequel of the years of strife. And this reconciling ministry was essential for the Seminary's future usefulness. Would-be students were being warned in some circles of the perils to their faith in this unbelieving institution, and of the difficulty they would encounter in obtaining a charge on graduation. One can scarcely exaggerate the bitterness in the atmosphere. Shortly after my ordination I happened to occupy a seat in a railway train with an Episcopal bishop from the West. We entered into conversation, and he asked of what Seminary I was an alumnus. When I told him, he turned and faced me and looking into my eyes said with emotion:

My dear fellow, like my friend Dr. Cuthbert Hall, you have far too kind a face to be a higher critic.

To this day there are sections of our country where Union is viewed with alarm by the devout. Preaching at a Lenten service in Philadelphia in the 1920's, an elderly gentleman in the front pew with a huge ear-trumpet followed me into the vestry, and inquired, "Are you the President of Union Theological Seminary?" When I admitted it, he went on to say: "Well, I want to tell you that I listened carefully to all your remarks, and did not hear anything objectionable." It was not uncommon, when preaching in James Chapel Sunday mornings, to have visitors, particularly from the South, speak to me at the close of the service and thank me for my appreciative attitude towards the Bible and towards our Lord. They had anticipated that the Bible would be torn in shreds and Jesus made light of or blasphemed. A young Methodist minister from below the Mason and Dixon line on his way to the Union Seminary Summer Session met his bishop and asked his blessing upon his program of summer study, to which the reply came:

I cannot give a blessing on your plan to spend a fortnight in that heretical institution; but I will pray for you.

If such hostility prevailed even in recent times, one can fancy what Dr. Hall encountered in the stormy 1890's. His serenity of soul and his gracious manners, coupled with his evangelical preaching, had a transforming effect on the minds of hundreds. Many of that generation went to their graves with distorted notions of Union Seminary due to the mendacious reports spread by its detractors; but Dr. Hall did more than any other man to leave an utterly different and wholly Christian impression.

In 1902–3 and again in 1906–7 President Hall went to Asia on the Barrows Lectureship. The first of these experiences was a triumphant tour. Dr. Hall's sympathetic approach to non-Christian minds, especially to Indians very hostile to the superior attitude of Anglo-Saxons, gave him a ready hearing. Crowds flocked to his lectures, and he was importuned for numberless interviews. Unhappily he returned from his second journey a very sick man and was spared only a few months.

## PROFESSORS AND PROFESSORSHIPS

### WILLIAM ADAMS BROWN

During the disturbed years of the controversy over Professor Briggs several important additions had been made to the Faculty. Dr. W. G. T. Shedd's retirement left vacant the Roosevelt Chair of Systematic Theology. The financial basis of this Chair had a history. An early friend of the Seminary was James Roosevelt. His grandson, James R. Bayley, had left the communion of his fathers, and had been trained for and ordained to the priesthood of the Protestant Episcopal Church. He became a devotee of the Anglo-Catholic Movement, and eventually went over to Roman Catholicism, becoming a priest in 1842, and secretary to Archbishop Hughes of New York. When his venerable grandfather died, it was found that in consequence of his grandson's defection, his inheritance had been diverted to Union Theological Seminary. Father Bayley had a conspicuous career and became Archbishop of Baltimore; his forfeited patrimony, although contested in the courts, was confirmed by them to its new purpose.

When Dr. Shedd retired as Roosevelt Professor of Systematic Theology, the Board first (1891) elected the Rev. Henry J. van Dyke, D.D., of Brooklyn to the Chair, but he died before he could take up his duties. Then the Rev. John Hopkins Worcester, Jr., a graduate of the Seminary in the Class of 1871, and a pastor in Chicago, was chosen. Dr. Worcester, a brilliant and cultivated man, served only a few months when his health failed and he died in 1893. During his illness the Board called on William Adams Brown, a graduate of Yale University in 1886 and of the Seminary in 1890, who had received the travelling fellowship and spent two years in German universities, to substitute for him. Dr. Brown had specialized in Church History and was originally appointed instructor in that field. The grandson of two notable figures in Union Seminary's past, William Adams and James Brown, he entered now on a career of conspicuous usefulness, not alone as a theological teacher, but as a figure in the Presbyterian Church and in the realm of education. In the Presbyterian Church he served on the Board of Home Missions and was an enthusiastic leader in plans for unifying the approach of Protestant Christianity to urban populations. During the First World War he became Secretary of the General Wartime Commission of the Churches. He was a member of the Corporation of Yale University. Moreover, he was a foremost leader in the Ecumenical Movement. Irenic in spirit, he strove in his thinking and teaching to conserve that which was of worth in traditional theology and to combine with it the newer insights of his own day. For many years his *Christian Theology in Outline* was used in seminaries on both sides of the Atlantic. He filled the Roosevelt Chair until 1930 when he was made a Research Professor until 1936 and then Professor Emeritus. Thereafter, he continued to assist advanced students until his death in 1943.

Dr. Brown was a prolific writer, producing books, articles and prayers, and was the devoted friend of many generations of his students. He took very seriously a theologian's task to instruct the Church. He was continuously looking over the field, and industriously giving himself to the preparation of books to supply voids which he noted. He produced a very comprehensive and useful brief book on *The Christian Hope* in 1912, which is more than a study of personal immortality, handles the Christian outlook on the world's future, and deals systematically with various doctrines held by Christians, such as Premillenarianism, Universalism, Conditional Immortality, etc. In all his writings the style is straightforward and clear, and he accords every topic sufficient treatment to mention all that can be said. It was this fulness of treatment, even to the handling of the obvious, which made his lectures sometimes wearisome. He had an orderly mind and his conscience would not suffer him to omit anything which seemed to him to belong in the category which he was discussing. He had an immense knowledge of books, and he put all their contents into pigeon-holes in his capacious memory, and drew on their contents in his teaching. Occasionally he was induced to abbreviate and get at the heart of a matter. Then he was at his best. None of his many books is more valuable than a short volume entitled *Beliefs That Matter,* in which he attempts to summarize in condensed form the main convictions by which contemporary Christians live. This book appeals to laymen and has been widely read. It remains a classic in its field.

A student who has since gone on into theological teaching says of Dr. Brown: "For catholicity of interest, persistent enthusiasm, and real liberality of spirit, we (I'm speaking of students now) prize his influence and his memory." One who graduated some twenty-five years earlier writes:

In the first decade of the twentieth century we theological students were seeking a new language for our preaching so that we could translate the doctrinal expressions of the past for the benefit of thinking people inside the Church and those who had been estranged from it. This was a permanent gain, for after one had learned to separate the truth from a particular expression of it, he could ever after adapt himself to changing needs. There was a danger that the attempt at simplification would lead to a watering down of the truth, and much of our earlier liberalism temporarily fell into this danger.

We started with Clark's *Outline of Theology,* and then moved into "Billy Dog's" own book which contained much the same material that was in his lectures. Since Dr. Brown's weakest point was his delivery, our possession of his thought in book form made us, I fear, somewhat inattentive; but his genial and kindly spirit triumphed over all handicaps of speech and he was able to give us the first ground work for all our theological thinking since. His strong interest in the Church was a steadying influence when we as budding liberals tended to be critical of it; and time has taught us the deep implications of his faith that the truth of Christianity is not something *thought,* but something *done* by a community that carries its living power from age to age.

In long retrospect it seems that our thinking was rather too comfortably adapted to those within the Church circle, especially the respectable middle-class part of it. Now we know what we lacked was the rugged sense of sin which required two world wars to generate in us again. We had a speaking acquaintance with sin, but sin was so respectable and well-dressed as to be scarcely noticeable. It was certainly nothing original and born in us; and our dealing with it was, so to speak, at arm's length —"supping with the Devil with a long-handled spoon" as Dr. Fagnani said in a Chapel talk.

We know that in his later years Dr. Brown was far more concerned with the relevance of Christianity to the world-shaking problems that came to involve us all, but we knew him when it was a much more simple thing to be a conventional Christian. Had the discussion method of conducting a certain number of class sessions been available, his rich experience might have been of more use to save us from some of the superficialities of the social gospel that was then tempting us to cut our theological corners.

A graduate of a later decade has said of him:

W. A. Brown was never a good lecturer; but I think we felt we were getting a pretty good general view of theology. The one big thing I got from him was the understanding that doctrines are attempts to express in words convictions which grow out of experience, and that although men may differ in the way they express their convictions, the chances are that they share the same basic faith because they have had not identical, but similar, experience of Reality. It gave me a key to understand people with much more conservative points of view than mine, and enabled me later to work happily with Fundamentalists—provided they did not want to go to war! I liked "Billy Dog" personally, and respected his erudition; but he didn't kindle enthusiasm in most of us for theology as such. I wonder if anyone could have done so at that period?

This is the vast difference between that generation, about 1911–14, and today.

Another alumnus writes:

Few men made more impression upon us than Wm. Adams Brown. (I remember Norman Thomas' remark, when he was pastor of that difficult parish in East 116th St., that the professor whom he recalled with most helpfulness was Wm. Adams Brown.) His theological lectures seemed to us often dull and pedantic, but amid our student bull-sessions we knew there was in "Billy Dog's" lectures certain peaceable fruits. And always his kindly manner and infinite patience, his squeaky voice and beaming countenance, drew us to him with real and lasting affection. And his teaching has stayed with us.

I remember one occasion when he was trying to question the class without indicating the answer he hoped to evoke. After struggling with it for a while as we became increasingly bemused, he came forward with a disengaging smile, and inquired mildly: "I wonder if any gentleman could tell me what I have in mind to ask?" There was a pause, and then, of course, a shout of laughter, and between us we got on with the question, after he had blushed like a girl.

Still another says:

It was the judgment of my classmates that his basic course in Systematic Theology was more valuable to them than any course they took. It was because through his course Christian truth became manifestly orderly, valid, credible and the key to life's meaning, replacing the confusion into which contact with rationalism and skepticism had thrown my inherited and collegiate religious views.

Still another testifies:

I came to the Seminary very "unsettled" because college experience had upset my Sunday School views of the Bible. Dr. Brown enabled me to get my bearings again. His method of teaching, especially in Systematic Theology I–II, was too formalized to stimulate much interest in theology on the part of most of us, but those who took his seminar on "The Idea of God in Contemporary Philosophy" got a different impression.

## CHARLES PROSPERO FAGNANI

In 1892, to supplement the work in Hebrew and the Old Testament, another graduate of the Seminary, Charles Prospero Fagnani of the Class of 1882, began teaching. Dr. Fagnani was the son of a celebrated portrait painter to whom many crowned heads and other notables of the period of Louis Napoleon had sat, and who had come to New York to carry on his profession. His son, educated in Paris, graduated from the College of the City of New York in 1873 and spent two years in the Law School of Columbia. For six years he taught in the city's public schools and acquired skill in his calling. He came under the influence of the Rev. Dr. Howard Crosby, one of the most learned pastors of New York Presbytery, and offered himself for the ministry. On graduation from Union Seminary he held two brief pastorates when his health compelled him to go abroad. On his return the Faculty sought his services. He was a thorough drillmaster in Hebrew, and always a man of surprising humor. No class that he taught could be dull, although much that he brought in might be remotely related to the subject in hand. Generations of Seminary students remember him with affection as a unique and refreshing character. He became in time Professor of Old Testament Literature and Exegesis. Retiring in 1926, he went abroad to spend his remaining years in France, dying during the Second World War in the occupied territory in 1940.

Dr. Fagnani could reach and hold groups whom scarcely another minister could interest. He was widely sought after as a teacher of the Bible. He used a blackboard skilfully. For some years on Saturday mornings he taught the Sunday

School Lesson for the following day and packed the room with Sunday School teachers. When the automobile was coming into use, the West Side Y. M. C. A. opened a course in driving and in the technical care of engines for would-be chauffeurs. Fagnani took the course with several hundred men and was asked by the Board of Management to follow each session with a Bible study. The atmosphere was unfavorable and the constituency not religious; but Dr. Fagnani chose sensational topics: "Running out of Gas," giving a study for twenty minutes on the New Testament doctrine of the Spirit, or "Are your brakes dependable?", a searching treatment of self-control. Sunday afternoons in the same Association he used to give a Bible address. One was advertised with the arresting caption: "What Ails Your Face," and turned out to be a study of the Transfiguration with the two texts "He was transfigured" and "Be ye transfigured." He noted three factors as effecting the radiant look on the face of Christ: (1) A lofty purpose—"his decease which he should accomplish at Jerusalem"; (2) Exalting companions—Moses and Elijah; (3) Prayer—the transforming comradeship of God. He had telling illustrations which he collected from newspapers, magazines and many sources. He salted and peppered his paragraphs with his Puckish humor, sometimes startling. The conventional were often shocked, but he got hold of many for whom no other speaker on religion had any appeal. In the prayer meetings of the Madison Avenue Presbyterian Church, which he attended faithfully, he would often seem outrageous. If the meeting were dull, as such meetings often were, he would rise, face a number of elderly women, and remark: "Mothers in Israel, listen to me, and you will learn something—an unusual experience for most of you." On one occasion, when an elder had followed Dr. Fagnani's remarks with a very conventional prayer, he rose and complained that "Mr. So-and-So has 'unprayed' all I said." Often he was provocative, and when others took to their feet to say that they had not come prepared to speak but the professor's words prompted them to reply, at the close of the service he would suggest a vote of thanks to himself for saving a meeting from its ordinary insipidity and for stimulating to speech those too diffident to take part.

A graduate of the second decade of the twentieth century described Dr. Fagnani's classroom:

His beginning Hebrew classes were unforgettable—the classes, not the Hebrew. His short distinguished figure in his doctor's gown crowned with his handsome head, with the luminous eyes and the carefully trimmed greying hair, mustache and goatee, would wander into the classroom with the stem of a rose between his teeth. If there were men working in the street, repairing the roadway or shovelling snow, he would call us to the window and discourse briefly about "the other half," often holding the rose stem with his teeth as he talked. Then he would return to his desk, call us to order, and laying the rose for all to see on his desk would launch forth into his effective drill of the various verb forms and vocabulary.

## ARTHUR CUSHMAN McGIFFERT

On the retirement, in 1893, of Philip Schaff, an encyclopedic scholar, writer and editor, a Swiss by birth and education, and internationally known, the Chairman of the Committee which prepared the American Revised Version of the Bible, the Board called from the Chair of Church History in

Lane Theological Seminary in Cincinnati, Arthur Cushman McGiffert, B.A. of Western Reserve University 1882, and graduate of Union Seminary in 1885 who had studied at Marburg and Berlin, at Paris and Rome. He had been the pupil of Adolf Harnack, whom he resembled both in theological outlook and in the clarity and crispness with which he lectured. He had a passion for truth, an incisive style, and set forth his views sharply without regard to traditional positions. For many years he was the outstanding lecturer on the Faculty and probably the most potent factor in shaping the opinions of his students. His classroom was an exciting experience. He had demonstrated his scholarship in a remarkable volume on Eusebius, contributed to the *Nicene and Post-Nicene Fathers,* edited by Philip Schaff, in which the reconstruction of the library used by Eusebius is a major achievement. In 1899 he published a masterly *History of Christianity in the Apostolic Age* which was at once hailed by scholars, and remains after a half century a valuable book, particularly for its interpretation of the thought of St. Paul. But hostile voices were at once raised because Dr. McGiffert had fearlessly applied historical methods to the investigation of New Testament books and institutions. Church folk in this country were not yet accustomed to this.

The Presbytery of Pittsburgh overtured the General Assembly of 1898 and asked action condemning this book:

In this volume the New Testament is very irreverently handled, no special supernatural guidance is ascribed to its sacred writers, the genuineness of more than one half of the books composing it is called in question, discordant and mutually contradictory teachings are declared to be contained in it and its authority as a divine rule of faith and practice is set aside. Further, in said volume great distinguishing principles of the Presbyterian Church and even fundamental doctrines of evangelical Christendom are denied.

It is the most daring and thorough-going attack on the New Testament that has ever been made by an accredited teacher of the Presbyterian Church in America.

To this Overture the Assembly replied:

The Assembly stamps with its emphatic disapproval all utterances in the book called to its attention by the Presbytery of Pittsburgh, not in accord with the Standards of the Church.

But the Church needs peace; the union of all its forces; the co-operation of all its members; a spirit of brotherhood and mutual confidence, so that it may advance itself with intense zeal and no waste of energy to its great, pressing and practical work of saving the souls of men.

The Assembly, therefore, deems it wise to take no action at present, in the earnest hope that Dr. McGiffert may be led to make a satisfactory explanation of his position in relation to the Standards of our Church, or in default thereof, peaceably to withdraw from the Presbyterian ministry.

Dr. McGiffert issued the statement:

The action of the Assembly, as well as the Overture from the Presbytery of Pittsburgh upon which that action was based, make it evident that many of my positions, together with the spirit and purpose of my book as a whole, have been seriously misapprehended. Such misapprehension I sincerely regret, and I wish here emphatically to repudiate the false constructions that have been placed upon my book in many quarters. So far as my views are concerned, they have been and remain, as I believe, in accord with the faith of the Presbyterian Church and evangelical Christendom in all vital and essential matters.

The agitation, however, continued, and several resolutions were introduced in the Presbytery of New York to which Dr. McGiffert belonged. It was evident that if an action for heresy were begun the outcome would be a condemnation; Dr. McGiffert withdrew and entered the Congregational ministry. When one compares this unhappy episode with a similar attack upon Professor George Adam Smith in Scotland a few years later, it becomes apparent how far behind Scotland, in ability to deal with the historical interpretation of the Scriptures, the American Presbyterian Church at that time was. The General Assembly of 1899 contented itself with issuing a deliverance in which it reaffirmed the inerrancy of Scripture, the doctrine of the two natures in one Person in Christ, the institution of the Lord's Supper by Christ as a sacrament, and the doctrine of justification "by imputing the obedience and satisfaction of Christ" to believers. With Dr. McGiffert's withdrawal, the case was officially closed in 1900.

Of McGiffert as a teacher, one of his students writes:

He was a fascinating lecturer, and we all looked forward to the hours of his classes. I took copious notes, which made what looked like good sense when I reviewed them, and in the strength of them made good grades. I confess I was not captivated by the intricacies of the Ante- and Post- Nicene Fathers' thinking, but the course McGiffert gave us on the development of modern religious ideas was a joy. He was so logical, so clear, so sure ("Nothing could be further from the truth!"), yet so modest with all, that I think we all rated him as tops.

A student some ten years earlier writes:

McGiffert was the finest lecturer I can recall of all the men at whose feet I have sat in this country and in Europe. He had a comprehensive grasp of the entire pageant of Christian thought, and he set forth with sharp clarity the new element in each thinker. To be sure, he was so interested in thought that we gained little knowledge of other aspects of the Church's life. Its leaders were *thinkers* mainly; but how delightfully McGiffert portrayed the traditional and the novel in each of them! In my day he, more than any other, molded our theology. I recall his seminars: I had one with him on New England Theology from Jonathan Edwards down through Horace Bushnell, and another on the New Testament period. We all worked hard on our papers, because of our admiration of McGiffert, and his comments were superbly enlightening. I can see him now as he entered the classroom at 700 Park Ave., murmured a brief prayer which few of us heard, and then embarked on his lecture in such carefully thought out sentences that our notes read like a book. One day a week he questioned us, and answered questions, and we had to report from time to time on our progress through his assigned reading—so many pages of Clement, of Origen, of Athanasius, of Tertullian, of Augustine, etc. Some of the Fathers fascinated me, and I copied on cards their *bon mots*. McGiffert taught us to go to the sources, and report men's ideas accurately. He was suffering at the time from brethren who misinterpreted him most shamefully. I recall a conversation outside the First Church in New York where his book was under discussion. One brother asked another what he thought the worst thing in it, and was answered "I don't foul my mind with such books." This non-familiarity with the document did not prevent his speaking at some length on the need of purging the Church of such heretical abusers of the New Testament. In my day McGiffert was the idol of the students, and the more studious they were, the more they prized him.

A graduate of the first decade of the present century recalls:

I look back upon Arthur Cushman McGiffert as the outstanding *lecturer* of my years at Union. He could unroll the history of doctrine like a scroll, which you could not only read, but get down in orderly sequence in your notes, and cram up for examinations under A...B...C..., and I..II..III.. even to 1... 2...3... It was not till I got to digging into Paul on my own, first in New Testament theology, and later in preaching, that I began to suspect the simplicity and sequence of his interpretations; neither Paul nor Luther was as systematic and orderly a philosopher as he made them appear; nor did any one category suffice for such explosive and profound prophets as they were . . . or for any one of the greatest religious figures; least of all our Lord Jesus Christ. I suspect now that both the clarity and the limitations of his mind appear here: they could catch and hold the *ideas* he dealt with, but the *dynamic* might easily escape a man who had so little sense for worship as he.

A distinguished ecumenical leader, a student in the second decade of this century, says of him:

We regarded him as the most brilliant lecturer in either Union or Columbia. To sit in his lecture-room was an exciting intellectual experience. His penetrating analyses in his "History of Christian Thought" seemed so complete that we tended too easily to accept his views on any subject as "the last word." His sympathies were generally with the "heretics." He often made me feel that Christian tradition was something to be viewed with skepticism. He tended to leave the impression that there was hope for Christianity and the Church if only they could adapt themselves quickly and completely to the latest scientific methods and conclusions.

At the turn of the century there were a number of scholars who were free in their use of the methods of historical criticism upon the narratives of the Old Testament but hesitated to do this with those in the New. This was particularly true of some who refused to investigate with these methods events mentioned in an ancient creed. Dr. Briggs, for example, while he admired Dr. McGiffert personally, did not share his views on many New Testament questions, and became increasingly hostile. In the first decade of this century he was on the point of going to the Board of Directors and complaining of Dr. McGiffert's teaching. Some of the members of the Faculty talked over the matter informally, and the President, Dr. Francis Brown, went to Dr. Briggs and represented how unfortunate it would be if he, by whom the Seminary had stood when he was under attack, should be the attacker of a former student and a colleague. Dr. Briggs felt strongly on the historicity of events connected with our Lord's career and referred to in the Apostles' Creed. He wrote an article in defence of the historic reliability of the narratives which deal with the Virgin Birth of Jesus. That had become a subject of much public discussion at the time, and Dr. Briggs, who had been the archheretic of the 1890's was sought after in meetings of conservatives to confirm their belief in this article of faith. One heard on all sides the opinion that Dr. Briggs was not the dangerous heretic men had supposed, so swiftly do points of theological discussion change!

## THOMAS C. HALL

The steadfast fight which the Seminary had waged for liberty of scholarship had been recognized by a number of its friends with generous gifts to its funds. Almost immediately upon Dr. Hall's assuming the Presidency, two new professors were elected to the Faculty. One was Thomas Cuming Hall, D.D., a graduate of Princeton University and of Union Seminary in the Class of 1882. He had held pastorates in Presbyterian churches in Omaha and Chicago, had shown himself sympathetic with the social movements in those cities, and fearless in espousal of those he deemed unjustly denied their share in the nation's wealthy heritage. He was appointed Professor of Christian Ethics, and he also offered courses in the Homiletic Use of the Bible. His views on ethical questions may be seen in the volume *Social Solutions,* published by him in 1910, and his Biblical scholarship is evidenced in the volume he contributed under the title *The Messages of Jesus* to the series, *The Messages of the Bible* published by Charles Scribner's Sons. Dr. Hall was a man of commanding presence, handsome and impressive. His lectures, like his preaching, were uneven. He could be eloquent, but at times discursive, and this lack of orderly arrangement hampered the effectiveness of his classroom work. His students, however, liked him and are grateful for his insights.

A student of Hall in the first decade of the century writes:

It was a breezy and refreshing experience to attend Dr. Hall's classes. We had just been introduced to Rauschenbusch and had begun to realize that there was something rotten in the state of our capitalistic society. Where Dr. Francis Brown had delivered the prophets from the trammels of an infallible book, Dr. Hall linked them up with the growing social conscience that was then trying to make up for the shallowness of liberal Christianity. The way Dr. Hall could utter the name "Amos," with a ringing tone and a blazing eye, made the market place of Bethel live again, and we saw the parallel between the ancient oppression of the poor and social evils just being revealed in our Western civilization.

It was hard to take notes from Dr. Hall because we liked to watch him in action with his great chest extended and his beetling brows reminding us of a prophet denouncing the shortcomings of the Chosen People. Whatever notes he had before him, he showed us how a man on fire can rise above them and make direct impact on his audience. It seems to me now that he illustrated the weakness of classes given over entirely to lecturing. We never had a chance to challenge any of his remarks or entice him into discussing any of the disturbing questions of the day. We were then on the border between the liberal-fundamentalist controversy and the emergence of the social gospel, and we needed to be talked *with* rather than to be talked *at*. That fault in the conventional method of teaching in seminaries tended to make a lecture a presentation of "inert ideas" which we did not learn to use in varying combinations to interpret the stream of events pouring through our experience.

Another student recalls:

There were two phrases, which he borrowed, and repeated often to illustrate what he meant by ethical responsibility: "We are carving in marble, and every stroke tells"; and "Everything men do is to be viewed *sub specie aeternitatis*."

## GEORGE WILLIAM KNOX

Dr. George William Knox, a graduate of Hamilton College and of Auburn Theological Seminary in the Class of 1877, was appointed Professor of the Philosophy and History of Religion. Dr. Knox was a short and slim man with a limp, and of keen and brilliant mind. He had spent sixteen years as a missionary in Japan and had been regarded as a philosophical thinker of persuasive force. He had filled, among other posts, the Chair of Philosophy and Ethics in the Imperial University at Tokyo. He was a remarkable lecturer and preacher, who never appeared to have any notes before him and whose thought was poured forth with precision and order. His eminence may be gauged from his selection to prepare the article on "Christianity" in the eleventh edition of the *Encyclopaedia Britannica*. He was fascinating in conversation, and his books on Japan are delightful reading. He was a potent factor in shaping the thinking of students. His independence of current trends may be judged from the Taylor Lectures, delivered at Yale in 1903, on *The Direct and Fundamental Proofs of the Christian Religion*. His thinking was a refreshing break from the current immanentism which believed it could go "through nature to God." The God reached by this process, Dr. Knox insisted, was sub-Christian and could not be other than nature itself, ethically ambiguous. The Christian starts with God's finding him in Christ and then interprets nature by Him. The final demonstration must await the missionary crusade to bring every realm of existence under the sway of Christ.

A graduate in the early years of the century writes:

Dr. Knox and his gripping lectures seem a long way back from the turmoil in which we are living today. It is hard to realize how our minds were then largely absorbed with the problem of reinterpreting our faith from the orthodox expression into the so-called liberal thought. Some of us came to the Seminary with very little knowledge of doctrinal truths that we would be called upon to expound; and the conventional terms had very little meaning that we could make alive. We were desperately in need of someone who could penetrate beneath the old language and bring out truths new and old in terms that seemed to "tick." It is not uncomplimentary to say that we have largely forgotten what Dr. Knox taught us, for we have had to devise new ways to make religion live in the modern scene, but we can never dispense with the decisive technique which he illustrated for us. He showed how one can find contact with any sort of mind at any level, and make religious truth something real that carries its own weight of authority.

Another says:

No man on the Faculty did more for my theological education—and that is high praise for the Faculty of those years was a group of great teachers to all of whom I owe much. Coming to the Seminary from college where I had had no aptitude for philosophical thinking, it was a new and most stimulating experience to listen to Dr. Knox set forth with such keen reasoning the philosophy of the Christian faith. My religious life in college had been almost entirely devotional and practical, exercised largely in the work of the Student Christian Association. I came to Union to learn the reason for the faith that was in me, to undergird the faith of the heart with a faith of the head. And this, in his lectures on the Philosophy of Religion and in Apologetics, Dr. Knox brilliantly supplied. It was an inspiring discipline to sit in his classroom and to be held for fifty-five minutes at unfailing attention as he lectured to us on the rather abstract subjects of religious thinking which he made so vital. One can still see him and hear him as he sat before us with a finger against his face, his posture a bit contorted, and his voice at times a treble as he punctuated his reasoned discourse with the peculiar way in which he said "Of course"—yes, he almost sang it. He was ever willing with his personal patient and sympathetic counsel. Never have I met a mind of keener dialectic. His picture has hung on the wall of my study through the years, upon which I have often looked with deep gratitude and drawn from it renewed stabilizing inspiration.

A colleague of most exacting scholarship and guarded speech at the Seminary's Centennial in 1936 characterized him:

George William Knox, philosopher and man of affairs, schooled in the thought of the Orient, discriminating expounder of fundamental religious ideas, convincing lecturer, beloved by colleagues and students alike, a conspicuous name in the annals of this institution.

One of the most brilliant men in his classes writes of him:

George William Knox was, I am more and more convinced, one of the quietest, but most pervasive and permanent influences I encountered at the Seminary; and often, I can now see, because of *obiter dicta* that you never forgot. To this day I bless him for one sudden flash of such insight: "Gentlemen, never let yourselves forget that you are preparing for a profession that has two twin vices—laziness and conceit." Fosdick told me that he was equally grateful for a similar remark to their class: "Be very careful how you baptize the modern belief in progress into the Christian faith." He said that was his first eye-opener that led to his own *Christianity and Progress*. I remember likewise Knox's whimsical commendation of the student who wrote on his examination: "I believe in God; but *not* for the reasons suggested in this course." There was a tough-minded realism about his mind which made his flashes of deep insight the more revealing; and though I remember hunting him out at graduation time to tell him how much I owed him, I have come to realize in the decades since, that he laid some of the deepest and firmest foundations for my own faith in the living God.

## JAMES EVERETT FRAME

In 1897, James Everett Frame, a B.A. and M.A. of Harvard, a graduate of the Seminary and the Fellow of the Senior

Class of 1895, was appointed an Instructor in the New Testament. He was to serve until 1938, when he became Baldwin Professor of Sacred Literature Emeritus. Frame was a most thorough scholar, with an exacting academic conscience, and a painstaking teacher who faced students with problems of criticism and exegesis, and allowed no shortcut to answers. Painfully critical of himself and excessively modest, he produced far too little in writing; the volume on *Thessalonians* in the *International Critical Commentary* is his principal contribution in print. But over the years he had a vast influence on both his colleagues and students and particularly on those students who specialized under him. He took a prominent part in the services in the Chapel, where his carefully composed prayers were most helpful to worshippers on Sunday mornings. He was, as time went by, a very important factor in the policies and affairs of the Seminary, an embodiment of its traditions and a wise counsellor.

A student of his, later the occupant of a theological chair, writes of him:

Frame was a rigorous New Testament scholar. He was exact in expression, and his perception was correspondingly precise. He never indulged in easy solutions, but insisted that the essential thing was to ask the right questions. His aim was to teach the proper method rather than any results he had reached himself. Hence his lectures stimulated the enquiring student, and often irritated those avid for neat answers. He strove to teach without theological bias; and when he spoke with enthusiasm, it was rather to urge an "antecedent probability" (a favorite phrase of his) than to pronounce a convinced opinion. His commentary on I and II Thessalonians was a notable achievement, and turned the tide of scholarship in favor of the Pauline authorship of the second epistle.

Another student, subsequently a professor of the New Testament and still later head of a great univerſary, says:

Professor Frame impressed me primarily with two qualities. I put first his interest in and attention to the individual student. He would give an amazing amount of time even to those of us who were not too scholarly, talking about his subject, explaining to us in the simplest sort of language what the problems were in New Testament studies, reviewing his own thinking, and in a way asking us, immature New Testament scholars, what we thought of the several problems. His lectures were only a small part of his teaching. He was a man of great modesty, and he never attempted to hide from a student the difficulty which he felt lay in a problem, nor his own lack of certainty concerning it. You went out of his study feeling that at least for half an hour you had been brought to the very edge of critical study of the New Testament. He could even make you think for a brief period that you were as capable in the field as he was. Of course, if you really became too hypnotized and attempted to tell him your conclusions on the problem, he would begin asking you questions, and it would not be more than two or three minutes before you would have your feet back on the earth and realize that you had better get out of that office as fast as you could.

The other quality, of course, was his profound knowledge of the subject and his scholarly objectivity. Every slightest possible explanation of a problem had to be reviewed. There were no easy answers. He made you realize that you had met an individual whose scholarship was completely honest. He had no theological antagonists whose views he was trying to pull down. When it came to his work, which was the relationship in which I knew him, he was selfless in devotion to his task.

Another student writes:

"Jimmy" Frame, invariably so-called, is another teacher who

comes happily to mind. His small figure and unobstrusive manner, his innate modesty and almost shy ways, combined with his obvious scholarship to make him admired and loved. One remembers not only his classes, but the communion service he conducted with a simplicity and dignity that united heart and mind. His New Testament classes were never ended when the bell rang. As it rang he would murmur a word of apology at being interrupted, and then say: "But one moment, gentlemen, Luke 10:18: 'I saw Satan fall as lightning from heaven.' We don't know just what it means, but it is important. Do think about it." Then he would give us a gentle smile, and pick up his lecture notes.

Still another graduate, speaking of the deep impression Frame left on him, writes:

I always wondered at the massiveness of his scholarship and at his almost pathological passion for accuracy to the last detail. When he was conducting a class or a seminar or talking to you individually, I felt that here was a man whose desire for truth and devotion to it was like a flame in which any prejudice or partiality he might personally have had was burned away. It always seemed to me, not from his words but from his attitude, as though he were saying: "Let us sit down together at the feet of truth, and quietly listen and understand."

Another of his students, who became a professor in an Episcopal Seminary, writes of him:

Professor Frame was a meticulous scholar. He aimed at perfection in his own work, and he would tolerate no lower ideal in his students.

Like Socrates, he was a master in asking pertinent questions. By means of these he opened vistas through the woods, and he expected his students to go ahead in their search for the truth.

He took great pains to make things clear, and he was gifted with boundless patience.

Dr. Frame always insisted that all the available facts connected with a question should be sought out and carefully considered. Only in this way could a just judgment be formed. He was never content with easy solutions or half-truths.

## JULIUS A. BEWER

In 1904 two young men were added to the Faculty who were destined to long careers in the service of Union Seminary, Julius August Bewer and Henry Sloane Coffin. The first of these was a graduate of the Gymnasium at Düsseldorf and B.D. of the Seminary in 1898. He then went for further study to Basel, Halle, and Berlin, where he specialized in the Old Testament. On his return to this country in 1901 he was called to be Professor of the Old Testament Language and Literature in Oberlin, whence the Seminary invited him to be Assistant Professor of Biblical Philology. Subsequently, he filled the Davenport Chair of Hebrew and Cognate Languages. A fervid and eloquent lecturer, he made the prophets of Israel living factors for generations of students. His book on *The Literature of the Old Testament in its Historical Development* became a standard textbook in theological education. He was a devout man, always entering fully into the devotional life of the Seminary. The wars between the land of his birth and the land of his adoption tore his heart and he consoled himself with a pacifist position. He was ever a scholar and expected scholarly work of his students. One of his students, speaking of him in the classroom, writes that "he so identified himself with the prophet of whom he happened to be speaking that for us he seemed to be Ezekiel,

and we felt the prophet speaking to us." Another, now occupying a Chair of Old Testament, says what most impressed
him was that Bewer would plow his way through a half
dozen interpretations of a passage and arrive at one which
impressed the class as exactly correct. It was because Bewer
knew so well the background of prophetic thought, and especially the whole thought of the prophet whose oracle he was
interpreting. "To me he was the perfect exegete." Still another speaks of the reverent appreciation students had for
him because of the genuineness of his own faith. "When he
was dwelling on the faith of an Isaiah or a Jeremiah, and
fairly glowing with earnestness, we knew that this was also
his own faith."

Still another writes:

An unforgettable teacher, because of his great sympathy with
students and their personal problems, and because of his great
skill in expounding the Prophets, was Julius A. Bewer. His devout, one would almost say his pietist, nature met the needs of
many students in difficult times. To read several of the minor
prophets with him in Hebrew was a memorable, and has ever
continued a significant, experience.

Again another recalls:

His thunderous voice, reading a passage which had been
meticulously examined for authenticity, would boom forth "Thus
saith the Lord" with the conviction of the prophets themselves.
His was a rare combination of scholarly care with preaching
fervor.

Dr. Bewer retired in 1945 and died in 1953.

## GAYLORD WHITE

Gaylord Starin White, a graduate of Union in the Class
of 1890, after serving as minister of the City Park Church,

affiliated with the First Presbyterian Church of Brooklyn, took up the post of Headworker at the Union Settlement in East Harlem in 1901. At the same time, he became associated with the Faculty of the Seminary as Director of Student Christian Work. He was well known and loved by the Union students, supervising their field work in various parishes, settlements and similar religious institutions. Under him the Union Settlement had become widely known for the excellence of its ministry to its neighborhood and for the delightful fellowship of its residents. Mr. White was trusted and beloved by the social workers of New York City and served effectively as a connecting link between this rapidly developing profession and the Seminary. He was made Lecturer and later Professor in Applied Christianity. A very modest man, he shrank from lecturing, and did his teaching largely through personal interviews.

When Dr. McGiffert assumed the Presidency of the Faculty in 1917, he asked Mr. White to move up to the Seminary, placing on him responsibilities for many activities. It was a wise plan, for Dr. McGiffert's health was not robust and Mr. White relieved him of many of the chores in the administration. In 1924, he was made William E. Dodge Professor of Applied Christianity. He watched over the interests of the alumni and served as executive secretary of the Alumni Council and editor of the *Alumni Bulletin*. Later he was made Dean of Students, and as the demand for larger student participation increased, he organized and chaired the Student-Faculty Committee. He saw to the physical as well as the spiritual needs of the entire Seminary community, as Chairman of the House Committee. His charm, his tact, his Christian spirit always made him a unifying factor in the institution.

Like President Charles Cuthbert Hall earlier, he was zealous for a larger service by the Seminary to those beyond its student body. For many years, he directed the annual summer conferences for ministers and other religious workers; and when it was decided to inaugurate a modest Summer Session, it was inevitable that his colleagues should turn to him to organize and direct it.

Mr. White was so unassuming that few appreciated the amount of his contribution. One of the young instructors who was called to an attractive chair in a sister seminary reports that, although the President and various members of the Faculty and several of the Directors brought persuasion upon him not to leave, it was Gaylord White's quiet word of affection and advice which weighed most heavily for his decision to remain at Union; he is now one of the senior members of the Faculty. Mr. White's sudden death in November 1931 brought home to the Seminary community the extent of its loss.

## WILLIAM WALKER ROCKWELL

In 1905, William Walker Rockwell, a graduate of Harvard and of Andover Theological Seminary, with several years of graduate study in German universities, came as Assistant Professor of Church History to aid Dr. McGiffert, whose many students were taxing his never robust health. Dr. Rockwell had an extensive range of learning, and it was inevitable that he should interest himself in the Library. From 1908–13 he served as acting Librarian. But with the coming of Dr. Henry Preserved Smith as Librarian, he was made Associate

Professor of Church History, a post which he held until 1925 when he was made Librarian, retiring in 1942. He was an enthusiast for books. He startled and amused the Board of Directors by telling them that the growth of the Library necessitated much more room for the stack, and suggested that the entire dormitory (Hastings Hall) be emptied of students and turned into shelves for books. He added many valuable volumes to our collection by his constant watch over sales abroad and by frequent trips to see for himself what was being offered for sale. The wars and the consequent poverty brought important collections on the market, and he had his eyes out for purchases which we needed to complete our possessions in various subjects. His colleagues kept pressing him for current publications; but his major interest was in books already standard.

## HUGH BLACK

The Jesup Chair in preaching was filled in 1906 by the coming from the pulpit of Free St. George's, Edinburgh, of the Rev. Hugh Black, D.D. He had been an outstanding figure in the pulpit of the Scottish capital, the colleague of Dr. Alexander Whyte, and the writer of several popular books which had sold by the thousand. A queue used to form outside the church on Sunday evenings when Black was to preach, and at seven o'clock when the seat-holders were supposed to be in their places, a bell rang and a multitude of waiting people swarmed in and took all vacant sittings. His strong Clydeside accent and a vibrant quality in his voice rendered him even more effective as a preacher.

That Scots accent gave him an entrée to the most con-

servative pulpits in this country from which any other
preacher connected with the Seminary would have been
barred. He was much sought after by schools and colleges,
and soon became widely known all over the land. At the
Seminary he gave a number of courses and he devoted much
time to personal tutoring in preaching. Dr. J. R. Sizoo tells
how he came in once a week and Black let him preach to him
and gave him counsel. A member of the Class of 1913, who
has completed a ministry of twenty-five years in his last
charge, speaks gratefully of Black's capacity in his classroom
to communicate his enthusiasm for preaching. "We were
wont to feel that it is the most thrilling of tasks." He drew
a full congregation when he preached in the Seminary
Chapel. He was always a delightful companion and a brilliant conversationalist. He reached retirement in 1936, and
lived on at Upper Montclair until his death in 1953. He served
the Seminary well at a critical juncture in its life, and helped
to restore its good name and influence in many devout groups
in the land. Students liked him and found his Scots stories
most delightful. He had gifts as an expositor and a graceful
style of writing. *Friendship,* 1898, *Listening to God,* 1906,
*The Adventure of Being Man,* 1929, *Christ or Caesar,* 1938,
are among his most widely circulated books.

A student who was in the Seminary when Black came and
has since become a very well-known writer on religious
themes and a professor of homiletics, sends me this impression of Dr. Black:

Hugh Black left an indelible impression on all the students
during my years at the Seminary. On the lowest level it was a
physical impression, etched sharply on the mind and heart. In
him a new planet swung into our ken. There was the sensitive,

sharply chiseled face, the penetrating eye which was itself an organ of speech, even his wonderful, ungovernable hair, through which he would run his fingers, seemed to take part in his eloquence.

To many of us I feel sure the great service of Dr. Black as a teacher was not in any detailed instruction in the making of sermons, their structure or organization. Many of us in the awkward squad could have profited by much more of that. But what he did give was tremendous. He was a gift to the imagination, a living demonstration of what a great thing preaching could be, a visible embodiment of a herald of God. He gave a new dimension to the vocation to which we aspired. We were thrilled by the arresting and carrying power of the preacher. He was not someone to imitate. No one could do that (though I must confess that I was tempted to let my hair grow long, and try to acquire a Scotch burr). The quickening stimulation remained a powerful force.

In part Dr. Black's great service was his moving demonstration of the resources of the Bible in preaching. He was preeminently an expository preacher in the high Scotch tradition. Some of his courses, that on *Jeremiah* for instance, were largely expository sermons. That was a very timely service. For in my days, many a young Demosthenes, under the weight of his growing wisdom, had come to feel that he could dispense with the Bible except for a formal salute at the beginning of a sermon. Having become men we had put away childish things, such as texts. We soared high among the generalities. Dr. Black knocked that nonsense out of our heads. He made clear that in slighting the Bible, we were living on husks, while there was food for real preaching in our Father's book.

He made the Bible dramatic and persuasive. Even his reading the Scriptures was a revelation, not forgotten. He read the Scripture with an intensity and force, as though they had never heard it before.

Another, the minister of a large Harlem parish, writes:

My recollections of Hugh Black are vivid, since I not only took undergraduate courses which he gave, but also many graduate courses. Professor Black was essentially an actor in the pulpit, in the best sense of the word. His fine feeling for the dramatic and the human and the esthetic, was manifest and sometimes overpowering, in that it created and communicated values which often are obscured in preaching. In the class he would begin by saying, "When I take my Bible, I pick a text, and then ask myself 'What does this mean to my life?' and 'How can I tell it so that other men will feel it to be God's will for them?'" Once when he was preaching in James Chapel, he used the story of the Syro-Phoenician woman as an entrance into the message. The climax came with this kind of statement: "I believe that this woman came to Jesus in the form of a great temptation," which of course may be interpreted in two ways. Evidently this was in Black's mind, to arrest the hearers' attention so that they might be led to deeper and more important spiritual truth.

Still another recalls:

To know him and to talk with him about preaching was like being led up a rocky mist-wreathed mountain and being shown glimpses through the mist here and there until finally you stood on the summit in full sunlight. He was a great expository preacher of the Bible.

## CHARLES R. GILLETT

Charles Ripley Gillett graduated from Union Seminary in 1880 as the Fellow of his Class, and after postgraduate study in Berlin returned in 1883 as Librarian. From then until his retirement forty-six years later, he served under six presidents in a variety of capacities, as Librarian, Instructor in Theological Encyclopedia, Registrar, Secretary of the Faculty, Dean of Students, and Alumni Secretary, retaining the latter position until his death at the advanced age of ninety-two in 1948. He was known and beloved among the alumni of the Seminary for more than half a century.

# CHAPTER III

# AN INTERDENOMINATIONAL
# SEMINARY

As already noted, the original Charter of Union Seminary provided that "equal privileges of admission and instruction, with all the advantages of the Institution, shall be allowed to students of every denomination of Christians"; and from the outset, the student body was thus interdenominational. However, for half a century, all members of the Faculty and Board of Directors were Presbyterians. After the severance of official ties with the Presbyterian Church over the status of Dr. Briggs in 1892, and Dr. McGiffert's voluntary withdrawal from the Presbyterian ministry in 1898, the Seminary became increasingly interdenominational in both leadership and outlook, although it was not until 1909 that the first non-Presbyterian was elected to the regular Faculty.

Some of the Directors, notably D. Willis James, were dissatisfied with the theological basis of the Seminary and eager to see it made truly "ecumenical." From its origin, the Seminary had exacted a vow of its Professors and Directors which was substantially the vow taken by Presbyterian ministers and office-bearers. It had been slightly modified in language over the years, but so late as the inauguration of Dr. Cuthbert Hall, it had read:

In the presence of God and of the directors of this Seminary, I solemnly affirm that I believe the Scriptures of the Old and New Testaments to be the Word of God, the only infallible rule of faith and practice; that I receive and adopt the Westminster Confession of Faith, in all the essential and necessary articles thereof, as containing the system of doctrine taught in Holy Scripture; that I approve of the Presbyterian Form of Government; and that I will not teach anything which shall appear to me to be subversive of the said system of doctrine, or of the principles of the said Form of Government, so long as I continue to be a professor in this seminary.

Mr. John Crosby Brown, President of the Board, and Mr. James sought the advice of Edmund Coffin, who was the legal adviser of the firm to which Mr. James belonged, and with his help they introduced an amendment to the Constitution of the Seminary, which substituted for this affirmation the following:

I promise to maintain the principles and purposes of this institution as set forth in the preamble adopted by the founders on the 18th of January 1836, and in the charter granted by the legislature of the State of New York on the 27th of March 1837, and accepted by the Board of Directors on the 20th of December 1839.

This amendment was given a searching discussion in the Board in a number of meetings and was finally adopted at the November meeting in 1904.

The frank freeing of the Seminary from its ties to Presbyterian doctrine and polity in order that it might serve all Churches at once awoke an enthusiastic response among its devoted friends. These Christians were all loyal Presbyterians and generous supporters of that Church's work but they had come to feel that the denominational divisions of Protestant Christianity were obsolete and hampering. They wished the Seminary they loved to serve even more widely in training ministers for all Churches. Mrs. William E. Dodge, asserting that the change to a broader basis was one with which her late husband was in complete sympathy, offered $120,000 to endow a chair in "Applied Christianity" to "prepare the students of the Seminary to render practical service in the world, along the lines of its social needs, especially among the poor and among those who are estranged from the religion of Jesus Christ." Morris K. Jesup announced his endowment of "a graduate professorship of preaching." He wished the appointment of

some person of established reputation for power and acceptance in the Gospel ministry, such person to devote his time in part at the Seminary to the instruction of ministers in the effective discharge of the preaching office and in part to the community at large in such Biblical preaching and teaching as may be desired.

The Rev. Hugh Black of Free St. George's, Edinburgh, was elected to this Jesup Chair in 1906 as mentioned above.

## THE SEMINARY AND THE PRESBYTERIAN CHURCH

There were still ministers and leading laymen in the Presbyterian Church who deplored the suspension of Dr. Briggs and the rupture between their Church and Union Seminary. They also were aware how costly that rupture had proved to the Presbytery of New York. Numbers of outstanding laymen had left its congregations and allied themselves with those of other communions. These peacemakers planned a reconciliation at the Presbyterian General Assembly of 1911 in Atlantic City; the following resolutions were introduced and passed:—

Whereas, the Union Theological Seminary in the City of New York was founded by Presbyterian sources, and

Whereas, some years past there developed a condition which led to the severing of the relations which had existed from the organization of the Seminary, between it and the General Assembly; and

Whereas, we are persuaded that there are in the faculty and in the directorate of Union Theological Seminary men who are in accord with evangelical Christianity as expressed in the standards of the Presbyterian Church in the U. S. A., and who are zealous for the growth of the kingdom of our Lord Jesus Christ in the world, and

Whereas, we believe that it would be a signal manifestation of the spirit of our Lord and Saviour Jesus Christ, who prayed that "all may be one," for Christian brethren under the gracious guidance of the Holy Spirit to remove all misunderstandings, alienations and antagonism, and to become vitally and aggressively united in the doctrine of our beloved Church in the work of bringing nations and the world to Christ, therefore be it

Resolved, that the Assembly authorize the Moderator to appoint a committee of nine, to consist of five ministers of whom the Moderator shall be one, and four ruling elders, none of whom shall be connected with the directors and faculty of the said Seminary with a view to the re-establishment of relations between the Seminary and the General Assembly on the basis of the standards of the Presbyterian Church in the U. S. A.; this committee to report at the next Assembly.

Those familiar with the history will see at once that these

resolutions were loosely, not to say inaccurately, drawn; but they were well meant. Professor G. W. Knox was a commissioner at this Assembly, and the resolutions were shown to him, but he wisely refrained from any comment that might seem to commit the Seminary. This special Committee on Conference with the Directors and Faculty was made up of David G. Wylie, D.D., William Hiram Foulkes, D.D., John R. Davies, D.D., and S. S. Palmer, D.D., ministers, and Louis I. Severance, the Hon. Henry D. Freeman, Elisha A. Perkins, and the Hon. Warren E. Settle, ruling elders. The Moderator, Dr. John F. Carson, was Chairman but asked to be relieved and to have the Committee select its own chairman.

The Committee met with the Directors, and at the Assembly the following May in Louisville reported upon its conference. Meanwhile, the enemies of the Seminary had not been idle and had succeeded in placing one of their number on the Committee when a vacancy occurred. Hostile articles appeared in the press, and at the Assembly in 1913 at Atlanta, Georgia, the atmosphere recalled that of the Assembly at which Dr. Briggs had been tried. Bitter attacks had appeared against Professor William Adams Brown and President Francis Brown. The majority report of the Committee was at once followed by two minority reports; the second by Dr. F. C. Montfort was made up of a series of assaults upon the soundness of the Faculty. In a speech, Dr. Montfort called Dr. William Adams Brown "a Hindoo philosopher." Professor Adams Brown, a nervous man, was seated next to the present writer, and wished to rise on a question of privilege and deny this charge. It seemed not worthwhile, for Dr. Montfort had gone too far and the sympathies of some were changing towards those whom he assailed. The Assembly adjourned before President Francis Brown had time to be heard. That night was extremely hot, and we three commissioners who were members of the Faculty got little sleep. In the early hours of the morning President Francis Brown came into the room where his two colleagues were sharing an uncomfortable bed and asked if he might read the notes he had made for his speech the following morning. We listened, but it seemed futile in that atmosphere, both physical and spiritual, to look for a dispassionate consideration of the situation.

In the morning, Dr. Francis Brown was heard, but one could feel that the Assembly was not open to a calm statement of historic fact. After the noon recess, one of the bitterest enemies of any modernization of theology, Dr. Mark A. Matthews of Seattle, took the floor, and moved that the Committee on Conference be dismissed. Then he moved that a new committee of seven be appointed to which the three reports and any other papers be committed, and this new committee was instructed "to make a thorough investigation of all the legal, ecclesiastical and doctrinal questions involved, and to report to the next Assembly." Dr. Matthews was a very tall man, generally termed "the lone pine of the Sierras." He had not been educated as a minister, but had studied Law and had become a lay evangelist in one of the Southern states. Thence he had passed into the ministry and was pastor of the largest church in Seattle, where he had made himself a species of ecclesiastical boss. He was a dogmatist and a literalist, an effective controversialist who gloried in conflict. It was patent that he had by his resolution transformed what began as a conference into an investigation, and the enemies of the Seminary were to have their day. Dr.

Francis Brown asked me to go to the Moderator, Dr. John Timothy Stone, whom I knew, and assure him that the Seminary wished to meet the Assembly's committee and furnish any information desired, but that if Dr. Matthews were made its Chairman, we could look for nothing but unpleasantness. Stone bade me tell the President that he would not appoint Matthews Chairman. However, Matthews was a man not easily brushed aside. He went personally to Stone, pointed out that he had drawn and offered the resolution, and insisted that it was customary to make the mover Chairman. Stone yielded to this pressure, for he was having difficulty in getting any one to serve on the Committee. Two, whom he appointed, Dr. George Alexander and Dr. Edgar W. Work, declined. In their places he chose Dr. Andrew Raymond of Buffalo and Dr. Joseph A. Vance of Detroit. He was endeavoring to render the Committee as strong and as fair as possible. The other ministers were Dr. Mark Matthews and Dr. Courtland Robinson, and elders Rush Taggart, George V. Massey and Frank J. Loesch. The Committee visited the Seminary and were shown everything for which they asked. The three ruling elders on the Committee went fully into the legal aspects of the Seminary's finances, and reported:

Under the Charter of the Union Theological Seminary, which vested in the Board of Directors, the duty, among others, of selecting professors and did not grant to the Directors the power to divest themselves of this duty, there arose a legal obligation on the part of the Directors personally to select professors to carry out the fundamental purposes of the institution, and any attempt to delegate this power of selection to any person or tribunal, in the absence of express authority in the Charter, would be of necessity *ultra vires,* and hence null and void. No such authority is found in the Charter. From this it follows that the compact of 1870 is not legally enforceable, and the action of the Directors of Union Theological Seminary in returning to the Charter method of selecting professors, was, in the opinion of your Committee, in conformity with their duty.

This vindication of the legality of the course taken by the Directors was not what Dr. Matthews wanted. Accordingly, at the General Assembly he undertook to show that the funds of the Seminary came from the Presbyterian Church and the action of the Directors was a violation of trust. President Francis Brown was sitting behind him on the platform, and when Dr. Matthews sat down the Moderator called on Dr. Brown to reply. Although an extremely reserved man who found public speaking an ordeal, Dr. Matthews' specious and mendacious presentaion had roused him. He began by saying that he wished Dr. Matthews were in front of him that he might look him in the eyes and tell him that what he had said was not true, and that Dr. Matthews knew when he said it that it was not true. He had been shown the sources of the Seminary's funds, and knew that their donors or their legal heirs were heartily in accord with the Seminary's Charter and approved the course which the Directors had pursued in maintaining the Seminary's independence of "ecclesiastical domination." It was as forceful and cogent a speech as the Assembly ever heard. Dr. Matthews did not attempt a rejoinder.

The whole episode of the attempted negotiations, and particularly Dr. Matthews' resolution calling for an investigation terminated in a clear justification of the Seminary. It could say to its foes with the ancient patriarch: "Ye thought evil, but God meant it unto good." The slanderous rumors which had persistently been circulated ceased, or where they continued, could be answered out of the Assembly's own Minutes.

In the early conferences with the first Committee of the Assembly, representatives of the Board and Faculty stressed the Seminary's desire to be related to the Presbyterian Church in the sense of serving it in the training of ministers; but saw no reason for a legal connection with the Church any more than for a legal connection with the universities in New York City where our students were often members of classes and their students came to classes at the Seminary. Further, it was pointed out that the Preamble to the Charter specifically mentioned that the projected institution would furnish the means of a full and thorough education in the subjects taught in the best seminaries in the United States and *"also embrace a thorough knowledge of the standards and discipline of the Presbyterian Church."* The question was raised whether the General Assembly wished some voice in the appointment of the lecturer on Presbyterian doctrine and polity, under whom candidates for the Presbyterian ministry would receive special preparation for their examinations for licensure and ordination. But the representatives of the Assembly were prepared to leave to the Board of the Seminary the provision for this special training.

The Board and Faculty undertook to see that candidates not only for the Presbyterian ministry, but also for that of other communions, should receive such special preparation as was required by their respective Churches. This has been faithfully fulfilled over the years, and no student without such course or courses is recommended to his licensing ecclesiastical authority. A series of lectures in Polity, representing the Baptist, Congregational, Disciples, Episcopal, Evangelical and Reformed, Lutheran, and Methodist Churches were appointed, as well as lecturers in Presbyterian doctrine and polity. As a rule, our students were fully prepared for their ecclesiastical examinations.

Nonetheless, there were incidents which kept the Seminary in the press, and stirred up strife. In the Presbytery of New York there were several survivors of the epoch of conflict who constituted themselves guardians of orthodoxy and badgered students. If the latter knew their Bibles and the standards of the Church, they could usually worst their inquisitors. In 1914 the chronic questioner, a Secretary of the Bible Society, asked a candidate whether he believed that Moses had seen God on the Mount. The reply was made, "I believe Moses had a genuine encounter with God in the mount." "I asked, 'Did he *see* Him?'" After a moment's thought came the rejoinder, "In my Bible it is written, 'No man hath seen God at any time.'" The questioner was halted in his tracks amid the applause of a delighted Presbytery. But the heckling (for it amounted to that) generally resolved itself into demands for a literal affirmation of the historic accuracy of some miracle narrative. The Virgin Birth of Jesus was the favorite theme. Candidates of real intelligence were careful to assert their faith in the Deity of Jesus but to remark that some scholars queried the historic reliability of the infancy narratives in St. Matthew and St. Luke; hence, they, not experts, could not make an affirmation in that matter with the same positiveness that they could on certain other events in the Gospel, such as the Crucifixion and Resurrection. At times this sufficed; but at other times one or two critics persisted in appealing from the decision of Presbytery to Synod and the General Assembly. This kept up an agitation in the secular and religious newspapers. There were similar defenders of orthodoxy in other communions, but the publicity of a presbytery meeting, especially in the metropolitan area, rendered Presbyterian students peculiarly vulnerable.

These challenges of the action of presbytery in licensing students who did not see their way to categorical affirmations on points in question among scholars reached the Judicial Commission of the General Assembly. This body never overrode the decision of Presbytery, but contented itself with referring to deliverances of the Assembly, and remanding the case to Presbytery for "appropriate action." The Presbytery kept its eye on the challenged candidate and reported to the next Assembly that he was fulfilling his ministry to their satisfaction. A few men were lost to the Church by this annoying process. But the hardy and loyal went on their way. One, a brilliant missionary in China, had to go out under the American Board (Congregational) but on the field he was assigned to a joint enterprise and worked there until his lamented death.

## THE ECUMENICAL LIFE OF THE SEMINARY

An interdenominational seminary obviously has greater difficulty in maintaining unity of spirit and purpose than one attached to a particular communion. This is true of the student body. Here Union has happily succeeded in conserving solidarity of worship. The daily morning chapel, a voluntary service, is very largely attended. It is conducted by members of the Faculty in turn, and the Choir contributes largely to the heartiness of the singing and to the musical perfection of the worship. The Lord's Supper is observed at least once every semester, as well as on special occasions, such as the opening and closing of the academic year, and most of the students and members of the teaching staff are present. The members of the Episcopal Church also celebrate Holy Communion according to the Book of Common Prayer once a week on Wednesday at an early service, as, in a recent year, did students of the Lutheran Church of Finland on Fridays. St. Vladimir's Seminary, connected with the Russian Orthodox Church in America, has been housed in the Seminary since 1947, and its Dean is now an adjunct professor in Union Seminary. Its students are welcomed both at the morning chapel services and at student-conducted services in Lampman Chapel. In earlier years, there were various student prayer meetings, and these continue on an informal and intimate basis in the student residences. More recently, these have been supplemented by services more formally arranged, but still under student control, in Lampman Chapel. The form is not of primary importance; the fact that corporate devotion persists assures the religious unity of the Seminary.

About 1908, Professor Thomas C. Hall complained that there was too great unanimity in the opinions of the members of the Faculty. In subsequent years no such complaint has been heard. When a vacancy has occurred in the Faculty, care has been taken not to elect anyone whose contribution would duplicate that of other members. In the 1930's, Professor Ernest F. Scott, welcoming new students, welcomed them to an institution where the members of the teaching staff had a high regard and affection for one another but often loathed one another's opinions. It has been necessary to emphasize that the Seminary's liberalism involved unity in loyalty to truth, and to Jesus Christ as the Truth, while expecting wide diversities in theological interpretation, in social outlook and in ecclesiastical opinion. For the past sixty years the Faculty in addition to its regular meetings for the transaction of business has held a monthly social meeting at which a paper on some theological or other serious interest has been presented and discussed with the utmost candor. Such meetings have not necessarily modified views, but have familiarized members of the Faculty with one another's positions, and made possible solidarity of purpose amid varying opinions.

Another chasm might easily have opened between the Board of Directors and the Faculty. In the nineteenth century, when both groups were smaller and when all were Presbyterians, Directors and Professors easily mingled and all were personally acquainted. But with the increase in numbers in both groups and the varieties of churchmanship and social outlook, solidarity has not been as easily maintained. Happily there has been a tradition that all full professors are invited to the meetings of the Board. They have no vote, but they may be called on to speak when they have light to throw on the matter under discussion; and all know the problems, financial or other, which the Board is confronting. Members of both groups became familiar with each other's faces, and at the close of the meeting there is opportunity for conversation. Since the opening of the Charles Cuthbert Hall Refectory it has become customary for Board and Faculty to have dinner together after one of the quarterly meetings of the Board. At the dinner, several members of the Faculty are called on to report upon the work they are doing and a member of the Board is asked to speak briefly on some phase of the Church situation or of the Seminary's influence. These evenings spent together have proved enlightening and have drawn both Board and Faculty together in personal friendship and in a feeling of oneness in a common task.

An immediate result of the change in the theological basis of the Seminary was the opening of its chairs to ministers and members of various communions. Hitherto, all the professors had been Presbyterians, or had become such on their inauguration in their chairs. The first representative of another ecclesiastical tradition was George Albert Coe, a Methodist, elected Professor of Practical Theology in 1909. He was followed by Robert Ernest Hume, a Congregationalist, in 1914, Harry Emerson Fosdick, a Baptist, in 1915, Dr. Foakes Jackson, an Anglican, in 1916, and so forth. In latter years, at least half a dozen Protestant communions have been represented within the membership of the Faculty. In the current year, there are ten—Baptist, Congregational, Disciples, Evangelical-Reformed, Lutheran, Methodist, Protestant Episcopal, Presbyterian, Russian Orthodox, and the United Church of Japan.

Nor has the Seminary hesitated to avail itself of the services of members of the Jewish and Roman Catholic communions. In the Seminary's earliest years, from 1838 to 1842, Isaac Nordheimer, an adherent of the Jewish faith, was an Instructor in the Elements of the Hebrew and the Cognate Languages, and in the German Language. And for nearly five and twenty years, from 1903 to 1928, Francis Carmody, a Roman Catholic layman, served most efficiently as Instructor in Vocal Interpretation and Public Speaking.

Mr. Carmody was a lawyer and had been Professor at the University of Notre Dame, later he had taught at the

Law School of Fordham University. He was an excellent trainer of the voice and its use. He did not make those he taught self-conscious, and he had an unerring ear for faults in enunciation. He could take a montonous voice and get variety into it. Without making men theatrical, he could render them much more effective in speaking what they had written. He kept reminding men that they "preach for a verdict" and taught them to marshal their arguments and give their evidence tellingly. He warned against ranting—"emotional reaction without supporting evidence." He taught his students to read the Scriptures with a genuine feeling for the content of the passage and the mood in which it is written. He became the friend of many students, joining them at table in the cafeteria where they happened to be eating, and was always interested in what they were doing and to what they were looking forward. His sympathetic criticism of sermons, with whose doctrinal content he must have disagreed, was noteworthy. Many a graduate of that epoch speaks of what he derived from Mr. Carmody.

## THE NEW BUILDINGS

For some years the Seminary had felt itself cramped for its work in its buildings on Park Avenue at 69th Street, and no larger ministry could be undertaken in those quarters. On January 26, 1905, it was announced that "a friend of the Seminary" stood ready to give a million dollars for a site and buildings near the new location of Columbia University on Morningside Heights. The "friend" was D. Willis James, who had instructed his lawyer, Edmund Coffin, to begin quietly to procure options to purchase thirty-six lots forming the two city blocks from 120th to 122nd Streets between Broadway and Claremont Avenue. A Committee of the Directors reported to the Board on the proposed removal. Mr. James' offer was accepted and the new site conveyed by deed to the Seminary on February 3, 1905. A building committee was named the following autumn, plans drawn and accepted, and work begun.

It was clearly understood that in moving to the neighborhood of Columbia, no desire was in the mind of the Seminary to become an integral part of the University. For some years there had been arrangements with New York and Columbia Universities by which Seminary students were admitted to university courses and university students to Seminary courses. On Morningside Heights it was hoped that these relations would continue. In his address at the laying of the cornerstone, Dr. Knox said:

> The Seminary maintains its independence, its cordial esteem for both Universities, and acknowledges its lasting obligations to each, obligations which the future will increase beyond any possibility of repayment.

> And yet the Seminary is convinced that it, too, has gifts for the University. The munificent givers of this land and of these buildings have confidence that sound learning aids religion and that the religious convictions which find expression here are of profound importance for the University. Without suspicion but with friendship, without fear but with hope, Seminary and University shall in the future, as in the past, continue their careers of mutual help and profit.

The new buildings were occupied in June 1910, and their formal dedication took place November 27–29, at which representatives of many universities, colleges and seminaries were present. But while this great expansion of facilities was taking place, death removed several of the leaders most responsible for it. Mr. James died in 1907, Morris K. Jesup in January 1908, President Cuthbert Hall on March twenty-fifth of the same year, and John Crosby Brown on June 25, 1909. These men saw the Seminary's land of promise from afar, but none of them was spared to have part in the dedication of the buildings. The venerable Dr. Hastings was present at the laying of the cornerstone in 1908, but died the following winter. As we entered the Chapel, a memorial to her husband by Mrs. D. Willis James and their son, Arthur, we seemed attended by invisible presences. President Brown insisted that the present writer preach the dedication sermon, and with this sense of those no longer at hand, the text was "Thou hast given me the heritage of those that fear Thy name." Despite the urging of his colleagues, President Brown also refused to give the address at the dedication of the buildings, but invited Dr. Briggs. He spoke on theological education, and like an apostle in the New Testament was "long preaching" and some of his listeners slept. One, a representative of an ancient Scots university, placed conspicuously in the chancel, slipped from his chair and had to be assisted up on it again.

# CHAPTER IV

# THE PRESIDENCY OF
# FRANCIS BROWN, 1908–1916

Upon the regretted death of President Charles Cuthbert Hall in 1908, Professor Francis Brown was elected President of the Faculty. He was absent at the time as Director of the American School for Oriental Study and Research in Jerusalem. Professor George William Knox was asked to serve as interim President, and on him fell the chief responsibility for the plans of the new buildings on Morningside Heights—a task which he admirably fulfilled. He was an able administrator.

Francis Brown was the son and grandson of distinguished educators. He had graduated from Dartmouth College in 1870, and just before his election to the Presidency of the Seminary he had been invited to become President of Dartmouth—a post which he found it difficult to decline. He had begun teaching at Union Seminary in 1879, and was recognized as a very eminent Oriental scholar. Oxford had invited him to become editor of its new Hebrew Dictionary in association with Professor S. R. Driver and Professor Briggs —a monumental work which after more than a half century remains standard. Oxford recognized his service by conferring upon him the degree of Doctor of Letters.

President Brown was a man of dignified and impressive appearance (his nickname among the students was

"Jahweh"). Extremely shy and reserved, he found ordinary conversation difficult but gave himself in devoted friendship to his colleagues and students. As a teacher he was solid and thorough, rarely letting himself become dramatic even when treating most spectacular scenes. In his personal religion he was reverent and devout, and his conduct of worship was painstaking and affecting. He carried an atmosphere with him which suggested the majesty of the Divine Presence. His learning was encyclopaedic and his theology, in contrast to much of the liberal theology of the day, was steeped in the awesomeness of the Hebrew thought of God. He adored Jesus Christ in whom he revered the fulness of the Godhead in bodily form. He was universally respected in the Church, even by those who differed with him theologically. He stood adamant for the liberal position, and was a faithful ecclesiastic, present at the opening of meetings of Presbytery and remaining until the final roll-call.

President Brown knew intimately and was loved by the leading Old Testament scholars in Britain and on the Continent. In a sense it was a loss to scholarship when he assumed administrative duties, for a volume on *Kings* which he had begun for the *International Critical Commentary* was never completed, and a series of lectures on a period in Old Testament history which he had delivered on one of the Seminary foundations was never made ready for publication. He did not easily commit himself on critical questions, but when he did there was a decisiveness about his judgments which gave one the impression of listening to a final verdict. He sought to make himself accessible to students, but his Jovian personality and extreme reticence made it hard for them to become frank with him. There were times when committees went to his office to take up some matter of Seminary life and became dumb in his presence. I recall occasions when students had been to see him and had failed to communicate their needs or complaints, when he would summon me and ask me to see them and ascertain what was on their minds.

Few men on the Faculty, however, have been so profoundly revered. A graduate who sat in his classroom in the years just before he became President of the Faculty has written of him:

Dr. Francis Brown left an impression on us of massive scholarship. His mind was as full of detailed knowledge as the Hebrew dictionary he was then writing, and it was poured out upon us like water over small-necked bottles. Every statement about the meaning of some important word or passage was documented with ten or more references, which I, for one, laboriously copied down for future use in the saving of souls. He represented to us the battle, then on the firing line, of historical criticism; and we gained the conviction that, if a man of such scholarship held on to his supreme faith through the shaking of the foundations, God would surely survive, shorn of some of His ancient trappings perhaps, but still a reliable God. Despite all that was over our heads and beyond our practical use as preachers, there was left from his teaching a deposit that became a permanent part of our manner of thinking, so that ever afterwards we were able to extricate from the lingo of antiquity the spirit and insight of the Hebrew seers and make them available for the people of our day. Year by year one has realized what an unspeakable boon it was to be delivered at that age from Biblical literalism, so that one could spend his life untangling the essential and enduring truth from all the twisted misunderstandings that beset earlier generations who had been bewildered by the unfortunate associations of Sunday School theology.

Dr. Brown was a solemn but deeply friendly man who gave us the feeling that any trifling with the Book of Books was a sin, and that God was far more strict than most liberal theologians.

One of his students who himself became a distinguished Old Testament scholar wrote:

From the very beginning I was strongly attracted to Francis Brown and soon came to recognize in him my leader and ideal. Since I had had three years of Hebrew before entering the Seminary, I was fortunate enough to be admitted at once into one of his special exegetical classes in Exodus where we were introduced into the methods of literary criticism. It was in 1895, the time when the so-called higher criticism of the Old Testament was at the centre of interest and the battle for its recognition in the church still raging. One of Dr. Brown's tasks was to help his students make the transition from orthodox to liberal, critical interpretation of the Bible. So he showed us how to distinguish the various sources by the differences of language, style and points of view, and he assigned to each of us sections to analyze for report to the class with all the pertinent arguments for every detail. We learned to face all the facts in minute and exact investigation, to estimate their significance and to see for ourselves the truth of the critical hypothesis. It was painstaking research for us, and the hours in class were often tense, for Dr. Brown demanded much. But we had in him such an eager guide, himself deeply interested in this study, that he carried us with him. We were indeed singularly fortunate in having one of the greatest Biblical scholars as our teacher, whose learning and insight, power of sound judgment and clear discrimination amazed and inspired us, and before the greatness of whose personality we all stood in reverence.

In his seminars Dr. Brown trained us more fully in critical exegesis, to see what the Bible itself says, without imposing our views upon it. He showed us the importance of textual criticism for this and the handling of its methods, for we saw that the text had not been handed down correctly in ever so many passages. To give us practice in critical exegesis, textual, literary and historical criticism, he assigned papers to us in which we had to give our interpretation and then sum up our arguments in the form of minutely exact propositions. These were discussed, every word being weighed most carefully, and finally put to the vote of the group. It was excellent training. We learned to see the importance of correct and exact use of every word in all our work.

These special classes and seminars were elective and chosen only by comparatively few competent students who were interested in this extra training. In the large required classes on exegesis the students had only to read and translate the Hebrew text and explain the grammatical forms; Dr. Brown lectured on the exegesis. It was for some of us an unforgettable experience to hear him expound Isaiah or Job. He knew the abundant exegetical literature with its varying interpretations, and he showed how exegetes had tried again and again to find the correct solution of corrupt words or passages, that often it had not yet been found, but that much could be learned from the exegetical tradition and better suggestions might come out of it. So he gave us the names of many interpreters with their readings. That was the usual method at the time. For the advanced student this was valuable; the ordinary student could well have done without them. But Dr. Brown wanted to give the best to all. He had to overcome a great handicap, for many students were not prepared sufficiently for his Hebrew courses. The elements of the language which they had learned in the junior year they had mostly forgotten during the long summer vacation, and the preparation for the class in exegesis became distasteful drudgery and required an excessive amount of time and energy without any apparent corresponding reward. So most of them took only what was required for graduation, foregoing the mental and spiritual discipline and enrichment of the special courses.

During my student days Dr. Brown gave only courses in Hebrew exegesis, prefaced by introductory lectures on the particular book. Later he gave them also in the Literature, History and Theology of the Old Testament. I wish I might have had them with him as a student. But I am profoundly grateful for the solid foundation he gave me by exact training. I owe to him more than to any other of my teachers, and I had very great teachers both here and in Europe. I still feel Dr. Brown's influence every day. As I look up from my desk, I see his noble picture on the wall. His kindly eyes look into mine, still guiding and inspiring me in my studies, quietly asking whether I come up to his expectation and justify his trust. Often I think of his moving prayers in class and in chapel, and now and then of the early afternoon in my student days when I went to see him in his study and on entering at his bidding felt the indefinable but intensely real sensation of the presence of God filling the room. Dr. Brown must have been praying, communing with God whom he loved with all his heart and soul and strength. Saint and scholar, one of God's true noblemen.

Another who sat in his classroom a little later has written:

God fulfils Himself in many ways lest one good teacher should corrupt a school. During the years I spent at Union there were three men at the head of the seminary, three great men, as different in gifts and personalities as men could be within the Christian ministry—Charles Cuthbert Hall, George William Knox, acting president, and Francis Brown. They gave a memorable demonstration of the varieties of Christian experience and endowment.

It is difficult to describe the impression which Dr. Brown

made on students. He had come back from Palestine to take up
the Presidency. To many of us it seemed that the Prophet Isaiah
had returned from the Holy Land. He had a commanding dignity, even an austerity, which induced awe. He looked to us
like one of the Major Prophets. And his manner often confirmed
that impression. He was never designed by nature as a "greeter"
of any sort. The massive erudition of the Brown, Driver and
Briggs *Hebrew Dictionary* seemed to set like an aura about his
head, and set him apart.

Yet it was not long before the quality of the man's mind
and spirit made evident to even the most backward of the
students that in him there was greatness passing by. There was
a quality hard to name, except by the vague word "Manhood,"
but impossible to miss. There was a massiveness not only of
scholarship, but of character, as undoubted and impressive in
our human landscape as a mountain peak. There was no note
of apology in his Christian conviction and experience. He gave
us a new sense of dignity and reality in the Christian ministry.
None of us can ever forget the warmth of his interest, his quick
sympathy, and his patience with academic stragglers in the
camp. I am sure the experience of many others was the same
as mine, that I never came out of his office after talking with
him on personal matters, trivial no doubt, without feeling a reinforced person, and that perhaps the battle was not all lost after
all. He set men on their feet.

I know I have forgotten all the Hebrew I ever knew, except
part of the alphabet and the first sentence of Genesis, but I am
grateful that I shall never forget the teacher of Old Testament,
who taught the Prophets, and was, by the grace of God, one
of them.

Still later, another writes of him:

Francis Brown was just—Jahweh! Shy and reticent, he didn't

know many of us personally, and in class he never warmed up
to his subject, as Bewer did, for instance. We respected his immense learning, and we knew that what he was teaching was
basic; but we called his course "Signal Practice" from the way
he had of giving chapter and verse references after every statement. Of course he did teach us important things about the
structure of the Old Testament, and we did like him, and felt
his gentleness and his integrity.

I never think of Francis Brown without recalling how he
began a devotional talk in morning chapel one day. He read a
passage, and then cleared his throat—"Brrrrmph. This passage
presents certain difficulties to the scholar. . . . But . . ."

A student in his early years as President says:

He was a handsome Olympian figure with his graying hair
and pointed beard and penetrating blue eyes and majestic bear-
ing. His fearsome and unbending rectitude and his surface lack
of humor impressed us deeply. It was legend that he once said
to our Class, amid a host of references to chapter and verse in
Isaiah that "King Hezekiah died in the year 696 verse 18." He
was somewhat confused by the roar of laughter that greeted his
statement, but chose to go on without inquiring why we laughed
—so intent was he upon the thesis he was maintaining.

President Brown's inaugural delivered on the evening of
the day when the cornerstone of the new buildings was laid
(November 17, 1908) is a noble and massive interpretation
of theology as the servant of religion.

This Seminary was founded and exists in the interests of
practical religion, for the uses of a practical ministry, and it is
theological to this end. . . . We contemplate not something less
than a full scientific study of theology but something more. All
the mass of scientific detail, all the rigour of scientific method,

all the thoroughness of scientific induction, all the insistence upon facts and the unwearying search for all the facts, and the refusal to go beyond the facts, with which the laboratory has made us familiar, belong in our study of theological truth. There is no easy road to that truth. It is an exacting pursuit. All who engage in it, seriously, must share in its processes, as well as its results. We cannot give our men results in nice packets and send them out to cure the world with our medicines. What they get in that way will always be a borrowed theology, and not their own. We can lead them toward our results, but they must take the path themselves, and learn how to possess their own souls. It is only the man who will share our search to whom the truth of God can come with the dazzling magnificence of discovery, as it sometimes comes to us. It is only through this earnest rigour of the process that theology can fulfil its service to religion.

Concluding that the source of religion is in God and that there are *first* revelations in the Bible and in Jesus Christ, he developed this lovely paragraph:

For the purest water you go back to the spring, if you can reach it. You must dip carefully and with judgment. Rough scooping may bring you leaves that were floating idly on the top—these quench no thirst—, or stir up sand that rests quietly on the bottom—harmless and even purifying until you try to drink it. It does not cleanse the spring to deny that these things are there. These things belong to the nature of the spring—a hollow in the common ground and open to the sky. But, with these things in it, it is still the water of the spring that gives refreshment and life.

Mrs. Brown, a charming German lady whom he had met when studying on the Seminary fellowship in Berlin, was warm-hearted and outgoing, and made the President's house homelike to students. Unhappily, Dr. Brown lived only eight years after taking up the office of the Presidency.

Shortly after President Francis Brown assumed office, the Seminary lost the President of its Board of Directors, John Crosby Brown, LL.D., a banker, a Christian of deep piety and fidelity, a lifelong tither, and a member of the Board who had been conspicuous in all the affairs of the Seminary since 1866 when he was elected to its membership. The Board chose as his successor Robert Curtis Ogden, LL.D., L.H.D., a merchant, a churchman, and an outstanding leader in Negro education whose sponsored trips through the South did much to acquaint northern men and women with thoughtful folk in southern communities and establish an era of goodwill. Mr. Ogden was a tall man of commanding presence and during his brief tenure of office he presided with dignity over Seminary functions and helped to make them memorable occasions. He had excellent judgment, was deeply religious, and was thoroughly imbued with the broad spirit characteristic of the founders of the Seminary.

## HAROLD TRYON

In 1908 a member of the Class of 1904 came on the Faculty as Instructor in New Testament and Church History, Harold Harrison Tryon. Born in Germantown, Philadelphia, educated at the University of Pennsylvania, becoming Fellow of his Class at Union, he studied at the Universities of Berlin and Heidelberg, and spent a year in the American School for Oriental Research in Jerusalem. On his return, he took up teaching at Union and was to remain a most faithful and useful factor in the Seminary's life and work for the next forty years. He gave a number of courses and is most happily recalled by students who began Greek under his patient and efficient instruction. Man after man bears witness to the thoroughness and fascination of his teaching. Meanwhile, as Registrar, he became familiar as none other with the individual students and planned their courses with them. In 1925 he was elected Secretary of the Faculty with the status of a professor. With objective impartiality he kept the minutes and recorded Faculty action. Students did not appeal from his decisions as Registrar and the members of the Faculty accepted with equal sense of his utter fairness his interpretation of Faculty rulings. Over the years the Seminary has been blessed with few men so gentle, so modest, so unassuming, and at the same time so efficient. He was the producer of catalogues and of the annual schedule of courses, and of much else that never catches the eye or brings praise; but it was all skilfully and accurately done. One who took his Class in New Testament Greek, writes of him: "He not only taught us Greek painlessly; a dozen of us liked our work with him so well that we formed a special class to read Plato in his apartment."

A student in Tryon's early years as teacher writes:

I knew him in connection with certain Greek and Latin studies that I was attempting in early Church History. There were only two or three of us in his classes—they were really tutorials. But I have a clear recollection of his utterly unpretentious nature, his thorough scholarship, and his patience with his students. By no means a man to be called a "personality," he left a deep impress of the matter dealt with and of the significance of honest study.

One of his former students writes of him:

There was always an element of paradox in the teaching of Harold Tryon. "Greek without tears" was the slogan passed about from student to student concerning his course in beginning New Testament Greek. The student was eased into reading the New Testament with a sense of enjoyment in the power he was gaining over the new language. But it was not the whole truth. The slogan suggests a quick and easy method which might have something superficial about it. And if there is any one word which could not be omitted if one were to characterize the method of this highly skilled teacher, it was his *thoroughness*. Every day's work was significant in building the solid and indestructible foundation for the days ahead. No significant detail was elided. Every construction must be understood and there was always time for full explanation if the student were slow to grasp the meaning. There was something rigorous and exacting in this thoroughness. But somehow the teacher was able to transcend, with a smiling assured assumption of its worthwhileness, the drudgery of learning to be accurate down to the last iota subscript or the most intractable irregular verb-form. There was a quiet urgency in the atmosphere of that classroom that made one very reluctant to make the same mistake twice.

There was paradox too in the speed with which one began to read the New Testament, and the atmosphere of leisure that pervaded the class room every day. The competence which one felt in passing from the beginning class to the second year class in Rapid Reading, or even into Greek exegesis, was often surprising to the student himself. There was never a sense of hurry at any given moment. Time was there to be spent for the needs of the hour. But without pressure of any kind, indeed almost without the student's perception of what was going on, ground was being covered at a speed that would be the envy of many a teacher of a language far less difficult and less foreign to

American ears than Greek. A slogan might be coined for this aspect of Harold Tryon's teaching. "Make haste slowly" would be appropriate if one understood that "slowly" never implied dullness. Every moment of every class hour was used to the full, and the hour seemed to slip away rapidly. But there was never a sense of pressure, or of haste that precluded mastery.

Again one might think of paradox in connection with the fact that Harold Tryon was most widely known for his classes in the Greek language. But those who had other types of courses with him perhaps wonder why his name was so closely associated with language teaching. Those who were privileged to have his courses in exegesis found an interpretive mind and spirit at work there that had the sure touch of genius in this field. But perhaps his students in the "The History of New Testament Times" have most to thank him for. Here was the historian who knew how to open every door that would lead to knowledge of, and participation in, an ancient culture. Political events are sometimes made the main fare of the historian's diet. But this historian searched religion, literature, the arts, the daily ordinary life of human beings—their houses, their clothing and food, their occupations and amusements—and brought the whole human scene to life. In this course the students were invited and were irresistibly drawn to share in its completeness the life of the New Testament world.

Pervading every classroom over which Harold Tryon presided were the scholar's rigorous standards that govern the search for truth. But embodied in the teacher himself, were the patience, unshakable good humor, the Christian tolerance that put the stringent demands into a dress of happy, shared endeavor.

## GEORGE ALBERT COE

George Albert Coe, a Methodist, Professor of Philosophy in Northwestern University, was elected Professor of Practical

Theology in 1909 with special responsibility for the teaching in Psychology and Religious Education. He had published two books—*The Spiritual Life* and *The Religion of a Mature Mind*—in both of which he had applied the findings of current psychology to religious living. In 1917 he published a large book, *A Social Theory of Religious Education,* which gave the main points of his teaching on the subject. After his retirement from Teachers College, to which he went in 1922, he wrote yet another volume, *What is Religious Education?* He had a way of making distinctions sharper than the facts warranted, and these kept him in the forefront of controversy; it is a question whether one can draw so clear a line between "transmissive" and "creative" education. It was this habit of Dr. Coe's which brought him later into conflict with his colleagues and certainly made much that he said unacceptable to those teaching in the churches. But he was a vitalizing and provocative figure, and during his earlier years in New York he exercised a vast influence over students and over many Sunday School teachers. He lived to an old age, dying in Claremont, California, December 9, 1951, in his ninetieth year.

Dr. Coe proved a magnetic teacher, with an incisive mind and equally incisive speech. One of his students, subsequently a teacher, writes of him:

Central in his philosophy and practice were two complementary commitments: a scientific attitude toward all facts and a loving attitude toward all persons. Out of these sprang his passion for social justice, and his conviction that the social issues of the present are "the call of God to our pupils." From these commitments grew also his insistence upon the "critical examination of present practice," which was the key to his power to motivate widespread and serious study. This he did in note-worthy fashion by his sharp distinction between "transmissive" and "creative" methods in Christian education.

A graduate in one of the earlier classes which he taught, writes:

Another controversial teacher was George A. Coe in Religious Education. A pioneer in his field, he brought into our curriculum a spate of new ideas about what was called the Sunday School. Many of us opinionated youngsters used to laugh endlessly in our bull-sessions over his teaching about *the* child. One young-ster said "Lock George Coe in a room with *a* child and open the door in an hour and that child would walk out leaving George Coe on the floor gasping." We ridiculed the instructions he gave us about the exact height of the chairs for a kindergarten child, or how much light should enter the windows of a classroom, as if religious education were wholly dependent on its setting. Doubtless now we have learned better and can see the values in a maturing movement in religious education, as we could not see them in its beginnings. But some of us, though properly chastened by George Coe's teaching and our own experience to back it up, still believe that the accent should fall on the Chris-tian in religious education rather than on *education* and equip-ment therefor. Still Coe is remembered for his contagious en-thusiasm, his tireless industry and his generous concern for his pupils.

An alumnus in a later class, says:

As a teacher he was top-notch. More than any other of my time he stimulated independent thinking. Some of his students were complete devotees both of the man and of his method. He made them feel that the use of modern educational processes was going to bring in a new day for the Church. On some I fear he left the impression that up-to-date techniques were as important as Christian revelation. He seems to me to have been the real "modernist" of my day in the Seminary.

## HARRY EMERSON FOSDICK

With President Hall's death, the question of the Practical Theology department came before the Board. President-emeritus Hastings, very elderly and frail, still lectured. He was well on in his eighties, but he met his classes until his last year in 1911. The Board invited Professor Arthur S. Hoyt of Auburn Theological Seminary to assume the leadership in the teaching in Homiletics. He had filled in when Dr. Hall went abroad in 1906–7, but he was unwilling to resign his post at Auburn. Henry Sloane Coffin, who had been Dr. Hall's assistant, was both too young to fill the Homiletics Chair and too busy in his pastorate to devote more than a few hours weekly to the Seminary. A young graduate, then pastor of the First Church of Montclair, was lecturing on Baptist Polity at the Seminary, and in 1911 he was also appointed instructor in Homiletics.

Harry Emerson Fosdick had begun his brilliant ministry in college pulpits, and his first books—*The Manhood of the Master*, 1913 and *The Meaning of Prayer*, 1915—were enjoying enormous sales throughout the English-speaking world and in missionary circles. He was an inspiring teacher of preaching. His students speak of his courtesy, shown in his unruffled manner when some unmannerly radical student spoke disparagingly on the financial basis of the Riverside Church of which he was at that time minister, his gentleness in handling the frailest type of sermon, his constructive suggestions as to the reordering and rephrasing of crude discourses, and his power of showing men how their work could be recreated. They dwell on his humility in placing himself in their positions, and viewing the homiletic task from their outlook when he had become the foremost preacher in the country. In 1915 he was appointed Morris K. Jesup Professor of the English Bible, and his lectures on this Foundation became so popular and were frequented by such numbers of visitors that the Seminary had to issue tickets to those wishing to attend. The contents of one of these courses were published in *The Modern Use of the Bible*, 1924. For a number of years he gave expository lectures for preachers and teachers on the *Book of Jeremiah* and the *Epistle to the Hebrews*. These have not yet been published, and they certainly should be. They opened students' eyes to the possibilities in expository sermons. Dr. Fosdick gave the Lyman Beecher Lectures at Yale in 1922 on *Christianity and Progress*. He took the morning Chapel service at the Seminary every Friday, and students from Columbia University and Barnard and Teachers Colleges flocked in along with the students of the Seminary.

Meanwhile Dr. Fosdick had become special preacher at the First Presbyterian Church, and was packing that edifice every Sunday morning. Unhappily, a controversy broke out over a sermon with the provocative title "Can The Fundamentalists Win?" which was given a very wide circulation. A complaint was laid before the Presbytery of New York, and was carried to the General Assembly. No decision was given condemning Dr. Fosdick's theology, but the First Church was told that it was irregular for a Baptist to be filling its pulpit steadily, and that Dr. Fosdick, were he proposing to continue, should be asked to accept the vows required of all Presbyterian ministers. This he felt himself unable to do, and to the extreme regret of his huge congregation he withdrew in 1925 after six years of most fruitful ministry. He spent a year abroad in the course of which he visited the Holy Land, embodying his experiences there in *A Pilgrimage to Palestine,* 1927. On his return, he accepted the pastorate of the Park Avenue Baptist Church, which later moved and became the Riverside Church.

In 1934 with the increasing responsibilities upon him in the Riverside Church, he resigned the Jesup Chair but continued to offer courses in Homiletics as an adjunct professor. Through all these years books poured from his fertile mind and pen. One, *A Guide to the Understanding of the Bible,* 1938, embodied lectures given at midweek services in the Church, and remains a very rewarding summary in popular form of the views of the Bible held by scholars in the first decades of the twentieth century. In 1946 Dr. Fosdick resigned his pastorate and at the same time retired from teaching—a sore loss to the Seminary and to the city of New York whose outstanding preacher he had been for three decades.

A former student, now a Professor of Practical Theology, writes:

Fosdick was a born teacher, a thorough, calculating workman. He knew what he was aiming at and went about it deliberately. Where many ministers would begin with a text, he would begin with a life-situation and often end with a text. When he preached on a topic we usually felt that he had said everything worth saying on that subject, as if he had presented us with an exquisite crystal globe in which was all the truth—nothing to add or take away. His teaching particularly reflected his own method which may perhaps be called the typically

American at its best. His graciousness with our fumbling attempts, his contagious enthusiasm for preaching, were irresistible. We arose to try again and again.

Another, at the Seminary two decades later, says:

Both in his teaching of the English Bible and of preaching, Dr. Fosdick contributed superbly to the development in students of usefulness for the Christian ministry. His lectures on the Bible gave new insights, while the rigorous discipline of his classes in preaching schooled them for careful pulpit work. While they were at first awed by his reputation and by what initially seemed a forbidding personality, they later found him a man of warm human sympathy, with a genuine interest in them as persons. His discipline in thorough work became a blessing.

On the occasion of his seventy-fifth birthday in 1953, through the generosity of Mr. John D. Rockefeller III, the Harry Emerson Fosdick Visiting Professorship was created to which is to be called each year a distinguished religious leader from any part of the world:

To honor Dr. Harry Emerson Fosdick for his distinguished contribution as teacher, preacher, writer and counselor, and to strengthen the training of the present and the oncoming leaders of the Christian church so as to enable them in their generation, as Dr. Fosdick has in this generation, to interpret the abiding truths and experiences of Christian faith in terms relevant and compelling to contemporary life.

## JOHNSTON ROSS

In 1912 the Rev. Professor G. A. Johnston Ross was called from a chair in the Presbyterian College in Montreal. He had held pastorates at the Bridge of Allan in Scotland, in London, in Cambridge, England, and in Bryn Mawr in this country, and was widely known as a preacher. He had an original mind, a distinguished mastery of English with the capacity to coin exact and memorable phrases, a sympathy which drew individuals to him for counsel, and a fervid Scottish temperament. From his arrival in the Seminary he was a force in its life. Sometimes he was in protest against prevalent trends in its thought, sometimes in fullest accord. He was never dull whether in the pulpit or the classroom. His students idolized him, and derived from him some of their most lasting preparation for their ministries. He was a popular preacher in many college pulpits, and sought after for student conferences. During the years when he was active in Union Seminary, its homiletics teaching led by Black, Ross, Fosdick and Coffin was recognized as unrivalled. Students from other seminaries came for these courses, and many were attracted to take their seminary work at Union. Ross continued as Brown Professor of Preaching for fourteen years, and remained as lecturer thereafter for four years more, when failing health compelled his resignation, and he spent his concluding years in Hawaii, dying in 1937.

He published a number of volumes of sermons and of lectures on preaching, all of which bear the marks of his penetrating insight into the Gospel and into the souls of men, and of the beauty and accuracy of his speech. He had the temperament of an artist and his moods were usually intense. This gave him force as of one driven by an inner compulsion, but his associates had to supply moderation and balance. Happily, they were linked to him with firm cords of affection. His service to the Seminary was so distinguished that its administrators did their utmost to keep him in a position to render it to the full. He was a mystic, finding his spirit at home in the Fourth Gospel and was constantly protesting the emphasis upon historic accuracy current among the students, who preached by preference on texts from St. Mark. This he called "barren Synopticism."

A student of Ross' writes:

Of all the faculty members of our time, Johnston Ross stood out as the most thrilling lecturer and the one through whom we came closest to the heart of the Gospel. . . . We left his classroom often in a state of rapture. Dr. Ross used the English language as a powerful ally; I remember in Chapel his snapping out the statement: "Jesus is more than a chubby bambino or a pallid cadaver on a cross." He spoke of the Jesus on stained-glass windows as a "bearded adolescent."

Another vivid description of his which is recalled is that of an afternoon tea, as a place where you beam "fatuously with tired cheek muscles on unknown people."

## PRESERVED SMITH

In 1913 the Board elected Henry Preserved Smith, D.D., Librarian. He was a ripe scholar, formerly Professor of the Old Testament at Lane Seminary, where the Fundamentalists had assailed him and had him removed from his Chair. He had then been called to Amherst, his *alma mater,* as pastor of the college church and Professor of Biblical Literature. Thence in 1907 he had gone for six years to Meadville Theological School, although he was not a Unitarian in creed. He brought to Union a wealth of learning, a keen sense of humor which rendered him delightful, sound judgment, and an established reputation for Biblical scholarship. At Dr. Francis

Brown's death, Dr. Smith assumed the Davenport Chair of
Hebrew and the Cognate Languages. Dr. Smith had published an *Old Testament History*, 1903, dedicated to Dr. Mc-
Giffert, whose colleague he had been at Lane, and in 1914
he completed his history of *The Religion of Israel*, dedicated
to Professor Briggs, who passed away before it reached publication. Smith's characterization of Briggs—"warm-hearted
friend, accomplished scholar, devoted disciple of the Master,
valiant defender of the faith"—is a striking reminder of what
this bitterly traduced scholar meant to his generation.

At the Seminary's Centennial in 1936, a colleague sum-
marized Dr. Smith:

> Biblical scholar of the highest rank, master of the historical
> method, lover of good literature, felicitous expositor of the his-
> tory and religion of Israel, gracious and godly in all his works.

The Seminary could not have found a more richly equipped
Librarian, for Dr. Smith was familiar not alone with his
special department of Old Testament studies, but also with
the entire range of theological learning, and his purchases of
books were always wise. He retired in 1925 and died a year
and a half later, in February 1927. A short book of Dr. Smith's
*The Heretic's Defense*, written with a lightness of touch
singular in the victim of venomous ignorance, says of his
prosecutors:

> Their most astonishing statement was that only an inerrant
> Scripture can have power to accomplish in the human soul the
> work for which the revelation has been given: that is, the work
> of conversion and regeneration. Since by the emphasis upon
> the original autographs the committee conceded that there are
> errors in the present text, they virtually confessed that our
> present Bible has lost the power of converting sinners. (p. 109)

## ROBERT ERNEST HUME AND
## DANIEL JOHNSON FLEMING

For the year 1911–12 Dr. G. W. Knox was given leave of absence to lecture in Asia. Accompanied by Mrs. Knox, he had a most useful journey, everywhere welcomed by missionaries and nationals, and fitted as few from this country to couch the Christian message in the light of Asiatic thought. But when he and his wife reached Korea, he was suddenly stricken and died at Seoul, April 25, 1912. His Chair, the Marcellus Hartley Professorship of the Philosophy and History of Religion, was filled by a pupil of his, Robert Ernest Hume, B.A., M.A., and Ph.D. of Yale and B.D. of Union in 1904, who had been born in India, had taught in the theological seminary at Ahmednagar and edited a Christian newspaper in Bombay. He was familiar with Sanskrit, and in 1930 he issued a translation of *The Thirteen Principal Upanishads*, which has gone through several editions and been hailed by scholars in that field as a first-rate piece of work. His *World's Living Religions* published in 1924 has gone through twenty-seven printings and continues in active demand. The University of Strasbourg gave him its honorary D.Theol. in 1932.

In 1918 the Chair which Dr. Knox had occupied was divided into three. Professor Hume continued to teach the History of Religions with the name of the distinguished Charles Butler, LL.D., attached to his new Chair. He became Professor-emeritus in 1943 and died in 1948.

To the work which Dr. Knox had handled as Professor of Missions, Daniel Johnson Fleming, B.A. of Wooster, M.A. of Columbia, a classmate of Dr. Hume's at Union, and M.Sc. and Ph.D. of Chicago, was appointed, first as Director of the

Department of Foreign Service in 1914, to which was added the Professorship of Missions in 1918. Dr. Fleming had been Professor of Science in the Forman Christian College in Lahore for eight years and was widely acquainted with the mission field in Asia. He has written many books to introduce the peoples of Asia to Christians in this country, and above all to stress the large contribution of the younger churches to our common Christian heritage. Some of his books handle realistically acute questions which confront missionaries—*Devolution in Mission Administration, Village Education in India, Sharing with Other Faiths;* others deal with ethical problems facing the missionary—*Ventures in Simpler Living, Ethical Issues Confronting World Christians;* others again treat the aesthetic side of the Church—*Heritage of Beauty, Each with his own Brush, Christian Symbols in a World Community.* During the Second World War the State Department asked Professor Fleming to serve as Consultant on India. Dr. Fleming prepared a delightful booklet, *Education Through Stone and Glass* which deals with the symbols on the doors and buildings in the Seminary quadrangle and the windows in the Chapel.

## FOAKES JACKSON

A Chair of Christian Institutions had been endowed and named in honor of the late Professor Briggs, and for several years the Seminary had been seeking a scholar of eminence to fill it. Dr. Briggs had made much of graduate study, and during the closing years of his service he had filled a graduate chair. The Morris K. Jesup Chair had also been designated a graduate Chair, and for a while the attempt had been made to constitute a graduate Faculty. But this was obviously a mistake, as graduate students sought out those professors in whose subjects they were interested or whose personalities drew them. So the graduate faculty had been abandoned after a few years. But graduate students in numbers were coming to the Seminary, and in 1916 the Rev. Frederick John Foakes Jackson, Dean of Jesus College, Cambridge, Canon of Peterborough and a foremost historical scholar in the Church of England, was called to the Briggs Chair of Christian Institutions. Dr. Foakes Jackson was a ripe scholar who had taught many branches of divinity and was a specialist in New Testament and Church History. At the time of his appointment he was engaged on a commentary upon the Book of Acts in partnership with Professor Kirsopp Lake. He published many books both before and after his arrival in this country. He was genial, witty, a delightful companion and a very learned teacher who could take advanced students and give them personal guidance in their chosen fields of investigation. He was sixty-one at his coming and always remained an Englishman. An Anglican in church affiliation, he was ecumenical in spirit, administered and received the Communion in the Chapel with his colleagues and the students, and took part both in meetings of Episcopal clergy and interdenominational meetings. He was also a lecturer for a period at the General Theological Seminary. He retired in 1933 and died on December 1, 1941. One of his ablest pupils writes of him:

He was genuinely devoted to his students, patient in correcting their essays, kindly but exacting in his criticisms. As a church historian he made his name with his *Introduction to the History of the Church to 461 A.D.*, and his combination of careful scholarship with balanced judgment and clarity, which marked that work, equally characterised his lectures. He knew how to simplify a difficult topic, to outline it, and to present it appealingly. In the classroom he had a lively and colorful manner and a ready wit, which he used effectively to unmask scholarly humbug.

## HARRY WARD

In connection with the difficulties which had come upon the Seminary in the First World War, the Rev. Professor Harry F. Ward of the Boston University School of Theology had taken the classes of Professor T. C. Hall. In 1918 he was elected Professor of Christian Ethics. Born in England, a Methodist, he had been headworker of Northwestern's University Settlement and subsequently pastor of several Methodist churches in the stockyards district of Chicago. The wretched plight of the underprivileged in this land of plenty had entered into his soul. He became a champion of social change. He was a fervent speaker much sought after for forums and other meetings on industrial questions. When he first took up his duties at Union he gave courses in the prophets and in the social teaching of Jesus. In 1929 he published *Our Economic Morality and The Ethic of Jesus.* A student of those years writes:

He communicated a degree of concern and a concreteness of concern for social problems which has meant a great deal to a great many students.

When the Russian Revolution occurred he became an attached disciple and later visited the Soviets and wrote on the new order with uncritical laudation under the title *In Place of Profit.* Dr. Ward was a moving preacher and a devout spirit; but as the years passed he became more and more committed to extreme radical social views, and the administration of the Seminary had more protests from various Church groups concerning his utterances than concerning all the other members of the faculty combined. He made himself difficult to defend by articles in which he declared liberalism outworn and impotent. Members of the Board asked, "Why, if this be so, should we protect him in the name of Liberalism?" In 1938, however, when he might have been retired at 65, the Board asked him to continue for three more years. In meeting the Board Dr. Ward thanked them heartily and remarked that he did not think there was another educational institution in the country which would show such forbearance and such devotion to freedom of teaching. His feelings were so engaged on behalf of those he deemed the oppressed that his lectures ceased to be completely objective. In most cases his students recognized this. He provoked them to think on the social questions of the time, and roused the complacent. During his earlier years at the Seminary he was a valuable stimulant—a flaming crusader for a more Christian order of society. He retired in 1941. A thoughtful and able graduate of the Seminary, looking back on Professor Ward's work writes:

> Union cannot expect to gather together professors who are constantly trying to understand the bearing of the Gospel upon every current of modern life without running the risk that some instances of extremism will find expression in its classrooms. It provides open debate and high scholarship which are the ideal means for helping a man get back on the right track if he has taken a false turn.

Another of his former students says:

In the course that I enjoyed with Professor Ward I was never at ease. His slow, low-voiced manner, added to his use of reports made by groups of students working outside the class hour, powerfully focussed attention and made us plough deeper than our *status quo* minds had been wont to do. He was ruthlessly honest and painfully probing. That he was a prophet I never had any doubt.

Still another writes:

Among the "wild Indians" of our day was Harry Ward. He was distinctly a controversial figure—inordinately admired by some and equally disliked by others. As a matter of fact it would be fairer to say that (like many others) he was too deeply sold on the idea that a change in the social order was the sole thing needed. Those who took his teaching as a half-truth got more from it than those who took it as gospel. Nevertheless much of his provocativeness had place in a heavily endowed institution dedicated to preparing men to work in the *usually conservative* American Churches.

# CHAPTER V

# THE PRESIDENCY OF ARTHUR CUSHMAN McGIFFERT, 1917–1926

WITH the death of President Francis Brown in October 1916, the Faculty met and asked the Board to appoint as acting President Professor McGiffert, and this was at once done. Then the Board set itself to consider the future leadership of the Seminary. The conclusion was reached that a pastor of experience should be sought. In turn, three pastors were approached; but none of them could see his way to leave his charge. The winter months rolled by, and the Faculty met again to offer their counsel to the Board. With unanimity they asked that Dr. McGiffert who had carried on the affairs of the institution admirably as acting President should be the choice for the permanent office. The Board decided to accede to the suggestion of the professors, and Dr. McGiffert was elected. His inauguration was set for the coming Commencement, and was made a simple ceremony in view of the War. Robert C. Ogden had died in 1913, and William M. Kingsley, LL.D., son of Ezra M. Kingsley, Treasurer of the Seminary from 1874 to 1900, was made President of the Board in his stead. Mr. Kingsley was a singularly felicitous speaker, witty, condensed, and sincerely devoted to Union Seminary.

President McGiffert in his inaugural dwelt upon the necessity of general culture in the preparation of ministers and upon thoroughness of professional training. The subjects in the curriculum have multiplied, but the length of the seminary course remains the same as when this Seminary was founded.

Had there not appeared a single new discipline in theology, the transformation of the old disciplines under the compulsion of the changed attitude toward authority would have required an increased amount of study in order to master the material as fully as it was formerly mastered . . .

Absolutism makes everything easy and is the perpetual resort of timid and indolent souls. . . . It is nothing short of a scandal that the professional training of a Roman priest should take longer than the training of a Protestant minister. . . . And if he be a liberal Protestant, who has broken with the authoritarianism of the older Protestantism, he ought to be still better trained.

He advocated at least four years of study.[3] Then, speaking of the varieties of Christian ministry and the need of preparation for all of them, he insisted:

Preparation for all these forms of ministry requires a common knowledge of Christianity, without which those that undertake any one of them will be but blind leaders of the blind. . . . The Seminary cannot make small men into big men, but it can give a knowledge of Christianity without which even the biggest man is utterly at sea in trying to bring Christianity to bear upon the problems of the world.

Then Dr. McGiffert went on to stress an aspect of the Seminary in which he was profoundly interested:

---

[3]The requirement of four years for the Bachelor of Divinity degree did not prove feasible, and was abandoned after a few classes had rebelled at it.

It fulfills in effect the function of a university Faculty of Theology, and as such it offers to every qualified person to study religion, and in particular the Christian religion, in all its aspects and for whatever purpose . . .

With the revolution that has come in modern times in the conception of authority in religion—the profoundest and most far-reaching revolution the church has witnessed since the second century—the spirit of independent scientific investigation can govern theological study as it never could before. We are not now obliged to ask what Bible or creed or church requires, but what the facts teach, and we are able to move in the field of theology with the same freedom that the scientist enjoys in any other field.

With the destruction of German leadership in learning due to the War then drawing to its climax, he foresaw the duty of American seminaries to provide that technical training for theologians and particularly for theological teachers, which Germany had so signally furnished in the previous half century and longer. He claimed this task for Union in the light of its history and present status. Finally, lest the stress upon the scientific spirit should eventuate in an attitude of neutrality to truth in its practical uses, he concluded:

Aiming to be a school of theology in the broadest possible sense, including within its curriculum every kind of subject that has to do with the understanding of religion, the Seminary remains, as it has always been, profoundly Christian. To serve the cause of Christ through the discovery and the interpretation of Christian truth and through the teaching and training of those who are called to Christian leadership, this it makes its chief concern.

This was no obvious remark. At the time, religious education was becoming increasingly free from Christian loyalties. To render Jesus Christ central and determinative was regarded as confining it to a stereotype of the past. The Bible was no longer the chief content of a school of religion. Within a few years a rift opened between Professor Coe and the President and Dr. Coe left the Seminary and joined the staff of Teachers College. While Dr. McGiffert was no churchman, and said next to nothing of the Church in his inaugural, he was standing steadfastly by the Seminary's Christian inheritance.

### FIELD WORK

In his inaugural address, President McGiffert dealt at some length with the question of Field Work, pointing out its value as stressed in the Preamble to the Charter, its necessity to most students for financial reasons, and its perils in interfering seriously with a student's scholarly work and not always contributing directly to his education. He announced that a plan had been devised which provided:

(1) assuring students such remuneration as they might receive for similar work under other auspices;

(2) securing the control and supervision of their work to the Seminary;

(3) finding enough churches and similar institutions willing to co-operate and furnish adequate opportunity for all needing this training.

In 1918, the Rev. Arthur L. Swift, Jr., (B.A. of Williams, M.A. and later Ph.D. of Columbia, B.D. of Union in the Class of 1916) was called as Director of Field Work. Mr. Swift's work in this Department soon gained widespread recognition, and men trained under him were asked to set up similar field work arrangements in other seminaries. In 1926 he was made Associate Professor of Applied Christianity, Professor Gaylord S. White giving over to him some lecturing. But it was clearly understood that the task of directing Field Work and rendering it educational to those who engaged in it was the primary obligation. In 1947 Dr. Swift was made Professor of Church and Community.

## EUGENE LYMAN

From its first days the Faculty had been enriched by scholars from New England. Another came to us in 1918 in Eugene W. Lyman to fill the Marcellus Hartley Professorship of the Philosophy of Religion. Born in 1872 at Cummington, Massachusetts, educated at Amherst College (B.A. 1894, M.A. 1903) and at Yale Divinity School (B.D. 1899), he was awarded its fellowship and studied for two years in Germany at Halle, Berlin, and Marburg. On his return he became Professor of Philosophy at Carleton College (1901–04) and was elected to the faculty of the Congregational College in Montreal (Systematic Theology and the Philosophy of Religion). He next served at Bangor Theological Seminary as Professor of Christian Theology (1905–13), when Oberlin called him to its Graduate School of Theology. And in 1918 we invited him to Union. A ripe scholar and teacher, a gentle and courteous and considerate man of devout spirit, he came at a time when following World War I a wave of "humanism" was sweeping over students and detaching many from Christian moorings. With acute sympathy, Dr. Lyman placed himself at their outlooks and patiently built up with them a Christian Theism.

An able student writes that:

Lyman lectured infrequently, and conducted his class by the discussion method.

He attributes the excellence of his results to

carefully prepared reading lists with specific assignments which introduced the class to the choicest chapters of the most valuable sources on the topic. There were small discussion groups led by students which were at times interesting, even exciting. Above all the secret of Dr. Lyman's success was his own personality, his belief in his students, his painstaking effort to understand and help them, and his high conception of the teaching office.

Another student speaks of his fairness of mind and intellectual honesty.

He represented a sane and thoroughly Christian type of Liberalism related to the contemporary mind, with emphasis on the relationship.

Still another reports of Dr. Lyman:

I learned a great deal in his courses because he set us all to reading; and he was so anxious to see all sides of every question that he steered me to material I might otherwise never have read. That he was a creative teacher cannot be doubted. The editors of *Liberal Theology* had on their hands a list of at least thirty of Lyman's students (not counting colleagues) who were teaching in the fields of theology or philosophy.

Still another recalls:

The benign, irenic spirit of Professor Lyman revealed itself in his teaching and in his counselling with students. Equipped with a thorough knowledge of historical philosophy and of contemporary thinking in related fields, his approach was comprehensive and his methods inclusive. Convinced that students should be compelled to think through for themselves the rationale of their faith, he required reading, thinking and discussion by the students before presenting his own lecture on a topic. He had a unique facility for drawing out from them the contribution each had to make to the thinking of the class. His personal conferences with them not only were tutorial sessions in developing a constructive philosophy of religion, but were also inspiring hours in helping them find themselves and their own possibilities for lives of Christian usefulness.

He married in 1926 Mary Redington Ely (Union, 1919) and together they made their home a hospitable spot for students, where informal talk did much to clear up mental difficulties. His stabilizing influence, particularly during the unbelieving postwar decade, was of immense service. His views at this period are well summed up in *The Experience of God in Modern Life*, three lectures delivered at Union just before he was chosen to the Marcellus Hartley Chair. The three themes with which he related the experience of God —the development of personality, social progress and cosmic evolution—disclose the major concerns of that time. He believed thoroughly in discussions in his classroom and welcomed frank expressions of student views, saw in them positive elements and sought to combine them in his syntheses at the conclusion of the hour. In 1928 he published his Ingersoll Lecture at Harvard on *The Meaning of Selfhood and Faith in Immortality*, and in 1933 a large work which embraced much of his thought and teaching on *The Meaning and Truth of Religion*. Dr. Lyman was an enthusiast for the Social Gospel, a sturdy opponent of militarism, and a

convinced liberal in theology and in politics. When he laid
down his work at Union in 1940, some of his colleagues and
friends honored him on his retirement with a book *Liberal
Theology*, of which he was a distinguished exponent.

## E. F. SCOTT

In 1919 Ernest Findlay Scott was inaugurated Edward
Robinson Professor of Biblical Theology. The Seminary
had sought him some years before, but he felt unable to
leave his Canadian post during the War. He had lectured
on the Ely Foundation upon *The Beginnings of the Church*
in 1914. Born in Durham County in the North of England,
educated at Glasgow University, Balliol College, Oxford, and
the United Presbyterian College, Edinburgh, Scott had held
a brief pastorate at Prestwick in Scotland, and then was appointed, first, Professor of Church History, and later, of New
Testament Literature and Criticism at the Theological College of Queen's University in Kingston, Ontario. He had
published a profound book on *The Fourth Gospel*, and another with original insights on *The Kingdom and the Messiah*.

Scott proved a delightful lecturer, clear, with short sentences unencumbered by the names of the learned from
whom he was drawing or by his own vast reading, with a
keen and subtle humor lightening heavier passages and a
provocative way of assailing his hearers' current idols. He
would give a sharp dig at that "pseudo-science, psychology,"
that "bag of tricks," current methods in religious education,
that "intellectually disreputable creed: the social gospel,"
that "half-wit, naked fanatic Gandhi" for whom he prescribed
hemp rope and a convenient lamp post at a time when paci-

fist students hailed him as saint and hero. The hours in his classroom passed swiftly and never without merriment. His book on *The Literature of the New Testament* contained the substance of his lectures in his introductory course. His nimble and incisive mind enabled him to take up subject after subject and become expert in it. He had been a pupil of Edward Caird's and was well read in philosophy. He mastered Spanish in order to read Ortega and Unamuno, but he never published on any subject outside his professional field of the New Testament and Church History. Dr. Scott aggressively espoused Franco when that leader was an object of execration at the Seminary. When the students asked him to address their forum, he chose for his theme: "Why is the American Climate Favorable to Freak Religions?" Beginning with two "distinguished female leaders" he dealt with Mrs. Eddy's cult and with "Mistress Aimee Semple MacPherson," remarking *en passant* that both ladies had domestic records into which it would not be proper for him to explore, and going on to say that "akin in intellectual profundity to the cults of these two widely followed ladies were the social gospel and religious psychology, whose devotees at Union were surprisingly numerous." The address was a *tour de force* which kept his auditors fairly rolling with laughter. Scott knew the pet themes of colleagues with whom he disagreed, and did not hesitate to hold them up to ridicule. Such an address cleared the air and "debunked" current student fads. While his language and manner were jesting, he was in earnest in his attacks and did greater damage with a clever rapier than could have been done with bludgeon blows.

He was an indefatigable worker and writer. The list of books which he published during his active days as Professor at Union is formidable, and each of them is a scholarly contribution to the knowledge of his subject. Each had a purpose. For example when Neo-orthodox colleagues made little of the historic Jesus on the ground that our knowledge of him was too scanty, and the adherents of Form-Criticism appeared to bolster this skepticism, Scott came out with a trenchant rejoinder, *The Validity of the Gospel Record,* 1937. His commentaries on *Ephesians, Colossians and Philemon,* and on *The Pastoral Epistles,* in Moffatt's series, and his books on *The Ethical Teachings of Jesus, The Epistle to the Hebrews, The Book of Revelation,* attest his thorough scholarship and his deftness in popular exposition. Scott became Professor-emeritus in 1938, and was at once invited to lecture and teach in various colleges and seminaries. He kept on writing and publishing valuable books, one of which *The Varieties of New Testament Religion,* is a most enlightening exposition of the diverse strands of thought brought together in the one relatively brief volume which the Church cherishes as the New Covenant. It is a fine contribution to ecumenical thinking making plain the differences in unity in the Christian Church from the outset. He has the distinction of having had more books chosen as primary Selections of The Religious Book Club than any other author. A student of the early 1920's recalls an episode in his seminar when a very competent paper was read on "The Eschatological Element in the Consciousness of Jesus." In the discussion which followed all the student comment was laudatory; but the Professor, contrary to his usual praise, tore the paper to shreds. The writer rejoined respectfully: "But Dr. Scott, I thought I was basing my paper principally on your own *The Kingdom and the Messiah.*" Unperturbed the professor answered: "Yes, but I've changed my mind since then." It is also recalled that at the farewell dinner given him by his colleagues, when someone spoke of his freedom from the interruptions of illness, he gave this formula for health: "Take no exercise, never sleep more than six hours a night; smoke continuously; and drink strong tea from the time you get up until you go to bed."

A discerning student of the 30's writes of him:

His lectures were models of lucidity, and his views were presented with such charm and balance that they left the impression there was nothing more to be said on the subject. Indeed, one wondered why there should have been any controversy in the first place. The solution seemed so obvious! Although a man of pronounced and even exaggerated opinions on current topics he was a patient and generous teacher, always ready to lend encouragement to the less talented student as well as to the more able.

Another student of whom Dr. Scott thought most highly says:

He was one of those brilliant geniuses whose lectures were nearly always exciting events. At first I felt that in every one of them he was making new discoveries in New Testament research. I came to see, however, that it was not so much a new discovery which he gave us as a new treatment of older themes which was brilliant in its critical judgment and synthesis. Thus he did give us new generalizations on old and ofttimes worn topics which were so convincing in form and unity as to make us feel that the problem was settled. Thus he gave us answers, while Frame gave us questions. The two formed a marvellous team.

Outside the classroom Scott was as exciting and interesting as at the lecture stand. He was an omnivorous reader, his interests ranging all the way from explorations in South America to Italian painters of the Renaissance. His comments and prejudices were always brilliantly presented. He was a man of books, and through books a man of the world, particularly the world of human beliefs, customs and thought.

## BRUCE CURRY

In the 1920's and 1930's there was no more popular figure at student conferences than A. Bruce Curry, Jr., Ph.D., a charming southerner who possessed unique skill as a teacher of the Bible. It was the epoch when "group discussion" was the vogue. Students supposed that when a group focussed its thought on a question or a subject, from within them wisdom evolved, and the result was "democratic" knowledge, supposedly superior to that furnished by any individual, however learned. Curry fell in with this current trend, propounding various carefully phrased questions and shaping the answers from his hearers as he placed them neatly on a blackboard. The result was satisfied listeners, amazed at their own powers, and prepared to receive the education offered because they had participated in the process of its formulation. Curry was a thoroughly trained Biblical student, a graduate of Davidson College in North Carolina, a student at Union Theological Seminary, Richmond, and Princeton Seminary, and an M.A. and Ph.D. of New York University. Few men were more successful in inducing students to look carefully at the pages of the English Bible and ask themselves: What is there? then, Why was it placed there? While he left his listeners marvelling at what he had evoked from them, he knew what he wished to communicate and carried them along with him. Curry had taught at both the Biblical Seminary in New York City and at New York University, 1913–25. Union called him as an Associate Professor of Practical Theology in 1925, and later appointed him to the Jesup Chair in the English Bible when Dr. Fosdick asked to be relieved of it in view of his heavy responsibilities in the Riverside Church. Curry's knack in familiarizing students with the contents of the English Bible and in helping them to become interesting and effective teachers of its books rendered him a valuable addition to the Seminary's staff. Unhappily, in 1936 he suffered a breakdown, resigned, and went to Southern California, where he lived very quietly and died in 1952.

A graduate writes of him:

He was an excellent bridge between what we were learning of higher criticism and exegesis and the use of such knowledge in the Church and Sunday School. Curry made religious ideas immediately *available*. We tended to be too sophisticated, too theoretical and too cold.

Another writes of him:

He gave his students familiarity with the English Bible and the ability to use it in teaching and preaching. Using the findings of scholarship, he saved students from mere scholasticism to an understanding of the several books of the Bible and the application of them to contemporary problems. Combining scholarly insight and educational technique, many found in his classes a practical synthesis of the other departments for the work of the parish ministry.

# CHAPTER VI

## THE CONTRIBUTION OF
## HENRY SLOANE COFFIN

BY MORGAN PHELPS NOYES

WHEN, in 1926, ill health made it necessary for Dr. Mc-
Giffert to resign the Presidency of the Faculty, the Board of
Directors turned at once to Henry Sloane Coffin as his successor. There was a certain inevitability about his election.
It could hardly be called a choice, for he stood alone as the
man for the task. Gifted, devoted, forceful, and already intimately identified with the life of Union Seminary, he was
the man raised up by God for such a time as that which
brought him to the leadership of the institution which he
loved. With a genius for friendship, a capacity for enlisting
the loyalty of young men, the tastes and heroism of the
scholar accustomed to terrible toil, an uncanny ability to
make clear-cut plans quickly and to carry them out with
despatch, a warm and dynamic Christian faith coupled with
evangelistic zeal, he was the ideal person to preside over a
Seminary training men for varied ministries in many denominations. He came out of the pastorate, having served since
1905 as minister of the Madison Avenue Presbyterian Church
in New York City, which under his leadership had come to
be regarded by many as the most effective church in America

from the standpoint of pulpit power, beauty of worship, institutional program, and pastoral services.

Dr. Coffin was no stranger to the educational world. For years he had been an influential preacher in college chapels, and in every generation of students at Union there were those who had been drawn to the Seminary because of some direct contact with him. Since 1922 he had been one of the "Successors to the Original Trustees" of Yale University. The President of Yale, Dr. James R. Angell, subsequently wrote:[1]

It is, I believe, no secret that at the time of Mr. Hadley's retirement several members of the Corporation were strongly disposed to restore the earlier practice of selecting a clergyman for President and urged that Dr. Coffin be chosen for the part. Other views prevailed, but no one can doubt that Coffin would have made a wise and effective leader of the University.

President Angell made the additional comment:

He brought to the Corporation broad experience in the Christian ministry and a wide knowledge of educational methods and ideals, both here and abroad. Few members of the Corporation have ever been the recipients of so many honorary degrees and these, be it said, from institutions of outstanding distinction, not only in the United States but also in England and in Europe.

Against this background of broad knowledge of education, Dr. Coffin had an intimate and thorough knowledge of Union Seminary. As he has indicated elsewhere in this history, his father had been attorney for certain of the Seminary's Directors, and was closely identified with the development of the present Quadrangle. He was a graduate of the

---

[1]*This Ministry: The Contribution of Henry Sloane Coffin,* edited by Reinhold Niebuhr. Charles Scribner's Sons: New York, 1945, p. 103.

Seminary in the Class of 1900, having taken his first two years
of theological study at New College, Edinburgh, an experience which gave all his subsequent ministry a certain Scottish flavor. He was appointed to the faculty in 1904 and for
over two decades had taught classes in Homiletics, Parish
Administration, Pastoral Work with Individuals, and the Conduct of Public Worship. His classes were large and enthusiastic, and few men were content to go through the Seminary
without taking at least one course of lectures under this
stimulating, devout and highly entertaining teacher. So easily
did admiration slip into imitation that it was sometimes said
that students who sat at his feet became "Coffinated." Each
year he had three or four students as part-time assistants in
the work of the Madison Avenue Church, and through them
he took pains to keep in close touch with the changing currents of student interest and opinion. He came to the Presidency uniquely equipped for the post.

It was in 1926—a difficult time in which to assume such
a responsibility for theological education. The period between
World War I and World War II was not a spiritually fertile
era. In the United States the reaction against the horrors of
war and the disillusionment with its aftermath had resulted
in a strong desire to withdraw from international responsibilities. Scientific humanism had led to the repudiation of
religious faith by many altruistic intellectuals, to a diluted
faith on the part of some who oversimplified the problem of
adjusting modern knowledge and religion, and to a militant
fundamentalism on the part of influential groups who sensed
danger in the newer outlooks, a danger which they thought
to escape by retreating into obscurantism. People were making money quickly and easily by speculation and in other

ways, and a growing belief that permanent prosperity had
been reached went hand in hand with lethargy in the spiritual life of multitudes. In the midst of growing wealth the
churches, engrossed in theological controversy, showed di-
minishing gifts for missionary expansion. Terms like "the jazz
age" and "the lost generation" were coined to describe the
life of youth, although any one in touch with the Student
Christian Associations of those days knows that there were
thousands of young men and women throughout the land to
whom the semi-decadence of the time came as a challenge
rather than as a lure. Dr. Coffin was admirably equipped by
training, temperament and abiding loyalty to the central
truths of the Christian faith for leadership in such a time.

Inaugural addresses, whether of public officials or of leaders in education, are proverbially untrustworthy indications
of what is to be accomplished by the particular administrations ushered in by such pronouncements. This cynicism,
however, is out of place with regard to the address delivered
by Dr. Coffin when he was inaugurated as President of the
Faculty on November 4, 1926. His inaugural appears in retrospect today as almost unerring in its outline of the emphases
and policies which were to characterize the twenty years of
his Presidency. No doubt this was due to the fact that those
policies had been maturing in his mind during the previous
twenty years of his intimate affiliation with the Seminary's
work. He had defined his theological position admirably in
1915 in an address to the graduating class with the title,
"The Practical Aims of a Liberal Evangelicalism." It is sometimes said that he completely changed the direction in which
the Seminary was moving and started it off along different
lines. Some of those who knew the Seminary best during

previous administrations and also during his leadership challenge that observation. He shifted the emphasis, but he did not change the direction. No words were more often on his lips than the statement of purpose formulated by the founders of the Seminary in the Preamble to the Constitution to which he refers in the first chapter of this history. By that compass he set his course, as had his predecessors before him.

In his Inaugural Address, Dr. Coffin described the threefold function of the Seminary as follows:

First, it is a training school for Christian ministers, recognizing the varied ministries for which our time calls, in the churches at home and abroad, in allied Christian organizations, in the teaching of Christian ideals and convictions in schools and colleges.

Second, it is a school for graduate study, whither those who have already received their ministerial training may come for further education, and where scholars may prosecute special research in some branch of Christian learning.

Third, it carries on what may be termed (in clumsy phrase) extension education in theology, offering training for workers in churches and kindred institutions, opening many of its courses to special students, conducting conferences for ministers and missionaries, and supplying through its faculty and occasional lecturers information and inspiration for the public.

With regard to the relative importance of these aspects of the Seminary's task, he stated his own position bluntly: "Of its three functions, all of them valuable, the first is the most important."

He was equally clear-cut in his description of what he believed should be the core of the curriculum for theological education. Declaring that in view of the variety of ministries demanded by the times, the Seminary ought not to insist on too rigid a uniformity in training for its students, he went on to voice his belief that there are three basic disciplines required by "all who intend to be accredited exponents of Christianity." These were "a thorough knowledge of the standard expression of the Christian faith and life in the Bible"; "a reasonable familiarity with the history of the Church"; and "a contemporary systematic theology—training a student in arriving at and stating his gospel in the light of today's thought and today's needs." Many who heard him were surprised when as a professor of Homiletics and Pastoral Theology he went on to say:

It is a mistake for students to devote a major part of their time to training in methods. A very modest number of hours in the class-room need be spent in such courses. Let the student apply himself to the basic studies which build up the content of his message; and let him spend several hours weekly under the sympathetic guidance of a skilled pastor leading older and younger folk into the Christian life. That is the theological education which equips ministers who last and remain fruitful their lifelong.

When Dr. Coffin reached the age of retirement in 1945 (and insisted upon retiring, although members of the Board of Directors urged him to agree to a suspension of the retirement rule in his case) it was obvious to all that his administration had, with remarkable consistency, been guided by the four ideals which he had set before himself and the Seminary in his Inaugural.

The first of these was the ideal of *scholarship*—"solid learning," as the Preamble stated it in words peculiarly congenial to Dr. Coffin.

The intellectual level of the ministry of our American churches, he said, is pathetically low. Recent controversies could hardly have arisen had our pulpits been filled with men abreast of current thought and seriously teaching their people. The number of college professors and leaders in the professions who show no interest in the Church is an alarming sign of the inability of our clergy to grip the minds and stir the imaginations of many of our educated people. A rift between teachers of religion and foremost thinkers along other lines constitutes a grave national peril. This Seminary must make upon its students a demand for scholarly work no less exacting than that expected in the best professional schools.

The second ideal was *churchmanship*. His churchmanship was not a mystic contemplation of an invisible entity called the Church Universal, although he was often called a High Churchman because he defined the nature of the Church in such lofty terms. (He has always spelled Church with a capital C.) He knew, was thoroughly at home in, and believed in the actual churches in cities and countrysides for which he was preparing ministers. He was acutely aware of the inadequacies of those churches, and declared that "we are eager to turn out men of venturesome spirit, unfettered by tradition, willing to risk experiments and to lead their congregations in a serious attempt to leaven their communities with the mind of Christ." Glorying in the interdenominational character of the Seminary, he taught men to play their parts loyally in the particular denominations with which they were affiliated, and to work for a united Church not by seeking the lowest common denominator, but by bringing together into one inclusive fellowship the "fullest faith and amplest devotion" of all. His election as Moderator of the Presbyterian Church in the U. S. A. in 1943 was a tribute to him by the particular Church which he loved and had faithfully served through the years, and brought to a climax his efforts to establish a warmer relationship between the Seminary and the Presbyterian Church.

The third ideal was *worshipfulness*. Here he found a need in the Seminary which he was supremely qualified to serve. Theological scholars do not always have the gifts essential for leadership in public worship, but Dr. Coffin was rarely endowed for this aspect of the Seminary's life. In his Inaugural he said that

the minister who would make worship appealing and enlarging to others must be himself a man of prayer, delighting in and ennobled by communion with the Father of our Lord Jesus Christ in the congregation of His people. He must acquire the art, a most difficult and complex art which embraces imagination, language, architecture, music—the art of expressing the longings and gratitudes and penitences of a group of folk feeling after a Wiser and a Better than themselves, and the art of affirming and making real the sufficiency of God. He must know how both for himself and for them, to throw wide the door into the presence-chamber of the Invisible, to face the Eternal Truth and Beauty and Goodness, the Source of power, the Wellspring of life, the loving Saviour of sinners.

This he himself was able to do for generation after generation of students. Chapel services which had been sparsely attended became central in the life of the Seminary fellowship. He believed in the importance of public worship, and it was no rare occurrence for a student casually reading the notices on the bulletin board in the corridor to feel a friendly hand on his shoulder and to hear a friendly voice in his ear reminding him in an outwardly humorous but deeply serious vein that his attendance at Chapel left something to be desired. At a farewell dinner given him by the Faculty at the time of his retirement, Dr. Coffin said that one of the things which he would miss most when he left the Seminary would be the morning prayers in the Chapel. This delight in worship he had communicated to many others.

The fourth ideal defined in his Inaugural was *a passion for the world-wide Kingdom of Christ*. As a pastor Dr. Coffin had been an enthusiastic supporter of missionary work. He had personally visited the pioneering work in China which he had persuaded the Madison Avenue Presbyterian Church to support. He had served on the Board of Robert College in the Near East, and was, throughout his Presidency, one of the most valued members of the Presbyterian Board of National Missions. "When we look at the cross," he said, "we can make no declaration less comprehensive than 'God so loved the world.'" "Whether our graduates stay in posts in this country or go to the ends of the earth, we would have them keep sight of mankind and every realm of its life as belonging to Christ." These were the ideals which Dr. Coffin set before himself as he assumed the Presidency, and these were the outstanding characteristics of his administration.

No sketch of his work as President of the Seminary would be complete which did not refer to his unusual ability as an administrator. He has described in this history the major developments of the Seminary during the period of his leadership but characteristically has made no reference to the fact well known to all who were closely associated with the Seminary during those years: namely, that his was the imagination, enthusiasm and administrative skill which were in no small measure responsible for them all. Only those within the Seminary family knew how many hours he spent with Faculty committees, giving his personal thought and attention to every detail of their work. The Seminary was fortunate in having an able Finance Committee of Directors and an efficient Comptroller during the difficult depression years, but they were fortunate in having as their ally a President of rare business acumen, whose Scottish caution did not hesitate to cut the budget to fit the dwindling income, and together they brought the Seminary through the critical years without a deficit in any year, a record equalled by few American educational institutions dependent for support largely on the income from endowments. Almost miraculously, the Seminary program continued to expand even though costs were rigorously cut.

It is, however, as pastor and friend to students that Dr. Coffin will be best remembered by the hundreds of men and women who passed through the halls of Union between 1926 and 1945 and by whom he was affectionately called "Uncle Henry." They were guests by two's and three's in his home for breakfast or lunch, where they enjoyed his good-natured banter, and then realized that in the midst of it he had found out what they were thinking and doing and hoping. If they were ill in the dormitory or in the hospital, they knew that it would not be long before they heard his knock on the door and found his reassuring presence in the room. His buoyant personality seemed to permeate the halls even when he was not visibly present. They knew that he was accessible if they needed counsel. They expected no sympathy with shoddy work and no toning down of the demands of the Seminary or of the Christian ministry and they received none. If there

were some who felt that he was too eager to have them accept
his judgments and others who resented the fact that he was
unwilling to accept their judgments on matters vital to the
Seminary and the world, few were unmoved by his searching Christian conscience and no one left his presence without
some access of spiritual vitality communicated by the President. When he first became President he would ask the direct
question of students and Faculty alike: "Do you pray?" He
denied dormitory residence to perpetual students who threatened to become built-in fixtures in the Library with no pros-
pect of ever putting to use the ever-increasing stores of
knowledge which they were laboriously accumulating. But
alumni returning to visit the Seminary from pastorates or
teaching positions could feel sure that his extraordinary memory would instantly recall their names and what they were
doing, and they knew that he was genuinely interested in
them. He was the actual Placement Bureau of the Seminary,
no matter where the responsibility for recommending men
to churches might officially be lodged, because it was to him
that the churches turned when they were seeking pastors,
and it was his mind and heart that were able most frequently
to find the right man for the place and the right place for
the man. There is no such thing as a perfect placement thoroughly satisfactory to all concerned (St. Paul seems to have
been unacceptable in several cities and critical of several
churches!), but Dr. Coffin struck a high average of success.
There have probably been few men in the ministry who have
preached so many ordination and installation sermons.

    At an Alumni Luncheon on Commencement Day a few
years ago the representative of a class which had graduated
five years before said in the course of his remarks: "Each

Saturday evening I read to my wife, who is also a graduate of Union, the sermon I have written for the next day. Sometimes she will say of one part of the sermon or another: 'I don't think Uncle Henry would like that.' So I change it." Probably Dr. Coffin himself would never have chosen to be what he has been to many of his former students, the invisible critic of their work as ministers. But it has been constructive criticism and the changes which have been made because "Uncle Henry wouldn't like that" have been changes for the better.

Two comments by Dr. Coffin's successor in the Presidency are in order. Referring to his staunch support of intellectual freedom in the Seminary, Dr. Henry P. Van Dusen has said:[1]

A convinced and determined liberal, President Coffin has stood immovably for full academic freedom. When members of his Faculty have fallen under attack for advocacy of unpopular causes, whether theological or social, and the opposition has sought to bring pressure through alumni or Directors, he has made their right to voice their opinions in accordance with conscience his cause, however much his views may have differed from theirs.

Quoting Dr. Charles Gilkey's observation that Dr. Coffin had been "the admiration of all of us, the model of many of us, the despair of some of us," Dr. Van Dusen, as he assumed the post which Dr. Coffin laid down, wrote:[2]

Dr. Coffin's colleagues of the Seminary Faculty, the ablest of the alumni, and his countless friends in the leadership of American Protestantism would reiterate that characterization. A quar-

---

[1] *Op cit.,* pp. 35–36.
[2] *Op. cit.,* pp. 37–38.

ter of a century ago in Scotland, Henry Sloane Coffin was widely recognized as the ablest allround minister in Protestantism—as preacher, scholar, leader of worship, pastor, parish administrator, church statesman. Few today would question the appropriateness of speaking of him as the ablest allround theological educator in America.

One of Dr. Coffin's colleagues on the Faculty who was closely associated with him in administrative duties, writes thus:

Shortly before his own inauguration President Coffin attended that of a President of a sister seminary. Upon his return he reported to our Faculty that an academic procession of distinguished representatives of other institutions had been kept waiting for over thirty minutes. He said that we must not allow that to happen with us, and thus established a tradition that academic processions at Union, no matter how large or elaborate, invariably moved within a minute of the scheduled time.

Dr. Coffin was a highly skilled administrator knowing how to delegate authority, and at the same time exact responsibility, pleasantly but firmly. He was careful not to interfere in the work of other officers of the Seminary. If it did become desirable that he should write concerning matters involving the work of others of the staff he would frequently bring to the Comptroller or Registrar what he had written to be "censored." He also made sure that the other administrative officers should be informed of what he was doing. This insured a smoothly working administration without misunderstanding.

From Dr. Cuthbert Hall's administration a service of worship had been held in the Chapel four or five days weekly. It was conducted by members of the Faculty in turn, and as it usually included a brief address it was easy for the service to run over its allotted twenty minutes and thus encroach upon the time of the first classroom lecture at nine o'clock.

One morning Dr. Briggs began his lecture promptly at nine to a group of students who had not attended Chapel. Several minutes later his lecture was interrupted by the entry of a larger body of students who came directly from the Chapel service. Dr. Briggs stopped the lecture, sat back in his chair somewhat helplessly, then resumed his lecture saying that he often had to protest against such excess of devotion.

Dr. Coffin resorted to more severe action when a service ran beyond nine o'clock. One morning from his seat in the chancel he directed the choir to begin the recessional hymn while the leader was still giving his meditation. It was resumed a week later.

He had a special gift as a presiding officer. Faculty meetings moved smoothly and rapidly—rarely over an hour. As the items on the agenda were taken up, the President would explain what was involved in each, and this would be followed by discussion, usually brief because if there was difference of opinion on an important matter, the President would have talked it over in advance with individual members of the Faculty in walks on Riverside Drive. Faculty meetings would at times move on too rapidly for the Secretary to keep an adequate record and compelled him to resort to the device of preparing in advance an abstract of the minutes, which could easily be filled in.

Members of the Board of Directors looked forward to meetings of the Board with pleasant anticipation, for the reports of the President of the Faculty never lacked interest—or humor.

The President's office had an atmosphere of informality. It was quite easy for members of the Faculty or students to secure an interview with him. If he was not engaged in a personal conference or committee meeting, the door between his room and that of his secretary's stood open. He usually recognized the voice of a caller at his secretary's desk and called out a hearty "come in" in welcome. Instead of waiting to ask a member of the Faculty to come to the President's Office for an interview, he would instead go directly to the professor's study whenever possible.

Early one morning a new student from the South arrived at the Seminary and found the main entrance closed. He walked around the corner to what appeared to be a private entrance on Claremont Avenue, dropped his luggage on the doorstep and rang the bell. It was much too early for the President's household to be active. Presently, a figure in shirt-sleeves, perhaps directly from the President's private study on the fifth floor, bounded down the stairs and opened the front door. Identifying the stranger at once as an entering student, he said, "Oh, you belong in the dormitory office," seized one of the student's cases and quickly led him across the quadrangle. As they walked, the student inquired, "Are you the janitor?" "No," was the reply, "but I try to be helpful to the janitor." When they reached the dormitory office, the attendant of many years, Mr. Emanuel Romero, arose in surprise to exclaim, "Why, Dr. Coffin!" The southern lad, with some consternation, protested, "But you didn't tell me you were the President!" "No," was the answer. "You asked me if I was the janitor, and I said I try to be helpful to him."

A prominent pastor who has recently become a Professor at the Seminary writes:

Very few students who sat under Dr. Coffin could have failed to realize that they were in the presence of a great and good and lovable man. His influence upon us lay in part in his own high conception of the pastoral ministry, a conception that shone through all his teaching. I for one can never forget the zest and enthusiasm with which he opened up the life of the ministry in all its aspects, giving us wise and kindly advice seasoned with his inimitable wit. His influence also lay in part in the wealth of learning and cultivation of mind that informed all his teaching. Here was one, we sensed, who had so given himself to the life of the mind and had so combined the role of scholar with that of pastor, that he unconsciously exemplified to his students the ideal he enjoined upon us. Still more, it was the heart and spirit of the man coming through his teaching, that won us. He not only *described* in his lectures what it was to be a faithful pastor; as he taught us, and mingled with us in the life of the Seminary, he *was* unto us as a pastor. His patrician breeding and manner were never a barrier to his own warm heart reaching out in friendship to all his students.

But it is the prayers of Dr. Coffin, his own strong faith kindling our faith, his reverence of thought and speech before the figure of Christ, that abides most of all in my mind. We all knew that what he said and was in our association with him, in classroom and chapel arose out of his own deep communion with God. One might apply to him the words he was fond of quoting from Pompilia's description of the face of the priest, Caponsacchi, in Browning's "The Ring and the Book": ". . . the brow that reverberated the truth, and flashed the word God gave him back to man." The face of Dr. Coffin, his personality, his character as he taught, will always be remembered as being like that by his students. Through him the world of the spirit drew near, and we knew that we were in the presence of a man of God.

Another alumnus, a well-known parish minister, writes:

My impressions of Dr. Coffin go back thirty years to the time when I was in my first year at Union Seminary. He taught us practical theology and introduced us to the fields of public worship and homiletics.

On one occasion a student presented an outline for an Easter sermon on a little-used text. Dr. Coffin was quick in his appreciation. Here, he pointed out, was the kind of preaching that would stir the interest of a congregation. A good text was half the battle. It was a principle which he followed himself and which he constantly commended to us.

On other occasions, he could be equally critical. A classmate of mine once submitted a prayer beginning "O Thou Infinite God of the atom." That was in the days when we were all struggling to reconcile the supposedly-conflicting areas of science and religion. Dr. Coffin could hardly wait to lay the offending phrase before us, much as a professor of anatomy might delight to stretch out on the dissecting table some new and unusual specimen. This, obviously, was not good prayer! His point was not made heavily, pedantically. It was done with his characteristic light, deft touch mixed with a generous element of teasing which removed any trace of class-room stuffiness or air of Olympian wisdom on his part and which made him a comrade in our efforts to become workmen who needed not to be ashamed.

His was a wholesome influence in the sense of keeping us from becoming cloistered and out of contact with the work-a-day world of the parish minister. At that time his seminary teaching was sandwiched in with a terrifically busy schedule as pastor of the Madison Avenue Church. Thus, when a student gave a rather sentimental sermon on "taking time to be holy," Dr. Coffin dealt with it first in terms of its homiletical virtues and defects. Then, as he disappeared through the door of the chancel on his way to his next parish appointment with coat-tails flying, he flung back over his shoulder a good-natured reminder that a minister had many other things to do besides being a "holy man."

Behind these snap-shot impressions, we gained the impression of the whole man—the faithful pastor, the competent preacher, the practical administrator who still found time to keep abreast of current literature as well as to retain his familiarity with the ancient classics. His lectures and class comments were liberally sprinkled with phrases from other languages—phrases which were sometimes facetiously corrupted by the students so that "Un façon de parler" became "a face on the payroll." On the other hand, I, for one, have had many occasions in the course of thirty years in the ministry to be grateful for Dr. Coffin's oft-repeated quotation "De gustibus non est disputandum." It was not just a sonorous Latin phrase. It helped to bring back to me the man from whose lips I had so often heard it and who enabled us to see that a Christian minister must be not only "alive to God" but broad, tolerant and understanding in his dealings with all sorts and conditions of men.

# CHAPTER VII

# THE PRESIDENCY OF
# HENRY SLOANE COFFIN, 1926–1945

## PAUL TILLICH

In 1933 the Nazi tyranny in Germany had worsened: books were being publicly burned, and scholars deprived of their chairs in universities. A committee was formed at Columbia to consider what might be planned for refugees who could be got to this continent. The Seminary was invited to be represented, and the President of the Faculty attended the initial meeting. We supposed that the deposed professors were all adherents of the Jewish faith and, then, it did not seem likely that the Seminary could find a place for them. A mimeographed list of the victims was circulated, and the question raised whom each institution in the city could contrive to employ and care for. The *Minerva Jahrbuch* was at hand so that we could identify each scholar with his subject. Towards the alphabetical end of the list occurred the name of Paulus Johannes Tillich, taken out of the philosophical chair at Frankfurt am Main. The President spoke up and undertook on the Seminary's behalf to provide a post for him, on condition that Columbia would also use him in its Philosophy Department, and provided he was able to employ English as a medium for teaching. Returning to the Seminary, the President looked up in the Library the books listed opposite Professor Tillich's name, and took out *Glaubensvoll Real-*

*ismus* to explore Tillich's point of view. Meanwhile Professor Niebuhr had obtained more personal information concerning him—the nature of Hitler's hostility to him, the size of his family, his academic record, and the probable date of his arrival should we cable him to come. The Faculty met, discussed the matter, and voted that each Professor should give five per cent of his salary towards a stipend for the first year. The Board of Directors proved sympathetic with the Faculty action, individually contributed towards the sum required, and voted him the use of a small apartment.

When Tillich arrived we found that he had been the first professor to be deprived of his chair because he had boldly warned his country that the Nazis would crush all liberty of investigation and teaching. He had been required to take the oath of absolute submission to Hitler, and on his refusal had been at once deprived. He knew a little English, his wife more, and their daughter picked it up with astonishing rapidity as soon as she began to attend school. Professor Tillich began at once with some German-speaking students to work away at his new language and made swift progress.

The Board gave him the title of Lecturer on Philosophical Theology; and he started to teach within a few months of his arrival, and while English was still to him a foreign tongue, he won the interest and admiration of students. We soon discovered what charming additions to our Seminary we had acquired. Tillich was not only a profound philosopher and theologian, but also a man of broad culture, intelligently interested in many phases of life—art, furniture, folklore, economics, social relations of all sorts, psychology, even the ballet. He had a devout spirit and a very tender heart. Refugees kept hunting him up, and he found it impossible to say

"No" to their necessitous pleas for financial aid. His heart was wrung with the miseries of his fatherland and he was asked to speak at many meetings where the German situation was discussed.

Columbia's Department of Philosophy found him too theological, and it became apparent that Union must assume entire responsibility for him and his family. This was no burden, for we had acquired a foremost thinker and scholar, and a man who captured the affection of colleagues and students. The Board promoted him to Associate Professor in 1937, and in 1940 Yale conferred on him the degree of Doctor of Divinity. In the same year the Board made him full Professor, keeping the title Philosophical Theology which fitted what he taught.

His courses became increasingly popular; invitations to preach and to speak at various meetings poured in on him; and before long one heard students talking of him as *"The Tillich."* His thinking was profound and the language in which he expressed himself, even in German, difficult because he felt obliged to coin new terms to clothe some of his views. It took students some weeks to become acquainted with his vocabulary. It was a concern of the homiletic department to warn against the use of abstract words. A very simple Brooklyn congregation listened to a sermon from a student which began with the declaration that "Christmas is the festival of the intrusion of Eternity into Time"—a sentence not likely to strike the average American as "good tidings of great joy." The fondness of the German philosophical mind for terms like "the Unconditioned" "the Abyss," or to describe the current situation under the Greek word *"Kairos,"* created barriers in the pulpit for those who became devotees of the

new Professor. Happily he warned them against the employ-
ment of his language in popular usage. He himself became
a very moving preacher in English, and his addresses in daily
chapel and his Sunday sermons drew unusual congregations.
He had a distinctive appeal for thoughtful persons who did
not find their souls satisfied in current American preaching.
The volume, *The Shaking of the Foundations,* 1948, contains
a selection of these sermons and addresses, and attests the
depth and passion of this truly Biblical preacher, prepared by
a unique experience to minister to a generation in tragedy.
In time he has become sought after by colleges where faculty and more mature students listen to him with rapt attention.

When one considers the constant demands upon his
time, the pains he had to devote to his teaching, the host
of his countrymen in distress who turned to him for counsel
and comfort, the number of his publications in English is
formidable. In 1951 the University of Chicago Press brought
out the first volume of his *Systematic Theology* which un-
folds his thought in orderly form and reveals him as a massive theologian—perhaps the most outstanding thinker at the
moment, whether one agrees or disagrees with his method
and conclusions. He often has spoken of himself as "a border
figure"—on the frontier between philosophy and theology and
between history and philosophy. It is a tribute to Union's
liberalism that it has accorded him so hearty a welcome, when
one considers how alien much of his teaching is to the point
of view which dominated the institution under Dr. McGiffert and Dr. George W. Knox. Respect for the integrity of
the man, for his courage in standing against tyranny, and for
his patient piety as well as the penetration and range of his

mind account for the admiration with which he is cherished by faculty and students. When in 1952 a series of volumes was inaugurated as *The Library of Living Theology,* Tillich was the first to be dealt with, and the fourteen essays, together with his own rejoinder, run to 370 pages.

One of his students has written about him thus:

Paul Tillich, driven out of Germany by Hitler, came to Union knowing virtually no English. Although he became quite at home there, to some students he always remained a mysterious, venerated man, of whom they knew only that he was immensely profound. Through many years Tillich never quite picked up the English idiom, and his struggles with the language were the source of countless anecdotes. As the perceptive foreigner sometimes does, he gained a marvelous ability to choose exactly the right English word; and the words and circumlocutions he sometimes devised were often more expressive than ordinary English.

The first impression Tillich made upon the student was likely to be that of a man of incredible scholarship and depth, thoroughly professorial in the best German tradition. He was, in fact, almost a caricature of a professor in a few details. E.g., he never ceased to be baffled by the intricacies of the Registrar's office, the counting of credits for degrees, and the necessary technicalities of an educational institution. To any question on these subjects he waved his hand helplessly, looked nonplussed, and referred the asker to someone else. Tillich perhaps never realized, though he was a grateful man, how much he owed to a few of his graduate students who helped him with administrative details, even to working over his manuscripts in great detail for publication.

In the classroom, too, he seemed professorial—at first. He seemed to read his lectures in a non-dramatic voice. Gradually students learned how deceiving this impression was. Actually the fires of German romanticism burned deeply in Tillich's inner being. He loved to teach. He commented once to a close friend, "Sometimes I am so weary that I sit in my office wondering whether I can meet my next class. But the minute I enter the classroom and see the students, I am tired no longer." He got a mighty exhilaration from teaching. The lecture notes which he seemed to read were actually scanty. Under the inspiration of the moment he expanded them greatly. Often, if questioned a day later, he could not recapture what he had said. To help him write his *magnum opus,* the *Systematic Theology,* students took lecture notes almost verbatim throughout an entire year, then arranged (with some co-operation from seminary authorities) to have the notes typed and presented to Tillich, who then had a basis for his book such as he had been unable to work out in his office.

Tillich was deeply poetic and mystical in nature. For some inexplicable reason Niebuhr and Tillich became closely associated in many people's minds. Actually the difference between their personalities and ideas was great, despite their mutual respect; and nowhere was it greater than at the point of the mysticism which Tillich so loved and Niebuhr so distrusted.

Students became fascinated by Tillich as they got to know him. Although he never developed any oratorical graces, classes hung eagerly upon his words; and in the pulpit he became a most moving preacher. One of the dangers in his teaching was that students became enthralled by him and tended to form a cult. But he was largely unaware of this and would not have wanted it.

He is one of the great philosophical minds of his generation. As a student I once commented to Dr. David Roberts that Tillich *almost* fell into every heresy in the book (except Arianism), but that he never quite succumbed to any of them. Roberts later repeated the remark to Tillich in my presence. Tillich laughingly and appreciatively agreed. The truth in the statement derived from his intellectual openness, his willingness to look for hidden profundity in any conception. It was all but impossible to ask a stupid question in his class, and Tillich never realized how stupid some of his students might occasionally be. Whatever the ignorance or denseness that prompted the question, Tillich would find in its language some significant problem.

When I was an instructor at Union, I once took our ten-month-old daughter up to my office, which was close to Tillich's. As we went past his door, he saw us and called us in. He seemed enchanted by the child. Then he said, in his weighty, almost mystic Germanic way, "If I could take this child to my class and the students could really *see* her, they would learn more than from all my lectures."

## RICHARD KRONER

Out of the black tragedy of the German situation another thinker came to us and joined the staff of the Seminary in 1942. Richard Kroner had held the Chair of Philosophy at Königsberg (The University of Kiel) made famous by Immanuel Kant. Kroner came of Jewish stock, although his family had been devout Lutheran Christians for several generations, and the bitter Nazi attempt to rid German culture of all its non-Aryan elements led to an invasion of his classroom by storm troopers who beat up his students, until the Professor could no longer endure the brutal treatment to which their connection with him subjected them. He asked and obtained a transfer to the University of Berlin although he was not allowed to teach there. Meanwhile his wife's mother, a lady of culture and wealth, the patroness of music in her community, was compelled to wear an armband with a huge orange "J" on it whenever she went out of her house. Professor Kroner could not eat the bread of idleness in Berlin, and he obtained through one of his former students, then high in Nazi circles, permission to leave the country, but not to take with him his books or any other possessions. He, his wife and daughter, went to Britain, where they had friends, and where he was invited to give the Gifford Lectures in St. Andrew's in 1939–40. He delivered them under the title *The Boundary Line Between Philosophy and Religion.* The Macmillan Company published them under the caption *The Primacy of Faith* in 1943.

On the basis of these Gifford Lectures he was invited to the Chair of Philosophy in one of the principal Canadian universities, and accepted. But war had now broken out, and a campaign was begun in the press of this Canadian city and carried on upon the campus against a German professor's coming. The Seminary's President received a letter from the Principal of this University describing the situation, saying that he was now incapable of carrying out his contract with Professor Kroner, and asking that the latter be met at the steamer in New York, and, if possible, that other work be procured for him. The United States was not yet in the war and the Principal expressed the hope that the same objections to a German would not prevail south of the Canadian border. We arranged to meet and take in Professor and Mrs. Kroner, and we spent an unforgettable evening in the social room where he gave us a moving account of his experiences under the Hitlerian régime.

We gave him the Hewett Lectureship on which he spoke not only at Union, but also at the Episcopal Seminary in Cambridge and at Andover-Newton, and repeated the series at McCormick Seminary in Chicago. They were published by Harper & Brothers in 1943 under the title *How Do We Know God?*. They are a potent statement of the necessity of God's Self-revelation in order to communicate true religious knowledge. Kroner says in his preface:

In order to show that this old and sacred testimony still holds good, I had to criticize a popular and widespread prejudice, namely the opinion that science is called upon to rectify, to augment, or even to produce the right knowledge of God. I felt this a necessary task the more because my German experiences taught me how dangerous all naturalistic tendencies are in the religious field. When belief in the sciences supplants belief in the Bible, the just relation between God and man is lost. As the sciences cannot deliver a real faith, all substitutes produced by them must dissatisfy in the long run. The final outcome, therefore, of a scientific criticism or reform of faith is a longing for a "new myth," that is exploited by ambitious and unscrupulous demagogues. When the true prophets are no longer trusted, not science but the false prophet will prevail in the end.

His treatment of faith recalled to some of us Bushnell's famous essay on "The Gospel a Gift to the Imagination." When publishing his Gifford Lectures, Kroner declared:

The tendency towards the humanization of religion is passing; it led finally to the dehumanization of man, and thus it refuted itself.

He calls his standpoint "a modern conservatism." It shows the legitimate right of a super-natural and even super-rational faith.

A former student writes:

Richard Kroner was one of Germany's great gifts to Union. In his years at Union he never taught any courses required for a degree, and he was not the sort to become a living legend like Tillich, so at first, relatively few students came to know him. Yet those who did found a magnificent mind and a wonderful spirit. On a few very able students he exerted the greatest influence of anyone on the Union faculty.

In his time he was the only unordained man on the theological faculty. Occasionally he would preface a remark with the statement, "I am a philosopher, not a theologian." There was no contempt in the statement. Renowned philosopher though he was, he did not believe in the powers of an autonomous philosophy.

The transition from Germany to America was a difficult one for Dr. Kroner. He had a brilliant reputation in Germany, but he came to America to find his greatest books untranslated and his name little known. Although a Gifford lecturer and a writer of several fine English books, he did not quickly attain in America the prestige he deserved; yet, after his retirement from Union, he was called to lecture in great universities from the Atlantic to the Pacific seaboards. Furthermore, he had come from the upper classes of Germany and was accustomed to the academic ways of the Continent. To adjust to the standard of living of an American professor (who had lost almost everything in emigrating) and the informal ways of the American classroom was a major change. To see how Kroner made it was a stirring lesson in Christian graciousness.

I once knew a young woman studying philosophy in New York. In conversation with a famous non-Christian professor in possibly the outstanding department of philosophy in the country, she heard him pour his scorn (fairly or unfairly) on the feebleness of philosophy departments in New York. Taken aback by his rebuke, she did not know whether she dared tell him that she was taking some work at Union, but she timidly explained, and was astonished at his reply, "Oh, that's different. Kroner and Tillich are real philosophers."

Kroner was utterly sincere and friendly. He was powerful and emphatic in his lectures, yet always ready to listen to the views of a student or to admit his own indecision on many an issue. In his years at Union students who came to know him learned to honor and love him.

In this connection an historian may record briefly other refugees for whom our Seminary proved a haven. When Czechoslovakia was menaced with invasion in 1939, a letter was received via Britain that the Rev. Josef L. Hromadka, Professor of Systematic Theology in the Jan Hus Theological Faculty at Prague, would certainly be sent to a concentration camp unless he could be rescued, and it was suggested that an invitation to speak in the United States might protect him, as the Hitler régime did not wish further to rouse hostility in this country which was not yet committed to a part in the European conflict. Accordingly, with the assistance of our State Department, an invitation was sent Hromadka to take part in the Summer Session. That proved impossible, but he gladly accepted and sent word of his availability for that autumn. He came, and we put his lectures on the announcement of courses for the first semester in the autumn of 1939. He proved a dynamic thinker and speaker. Students took to him at once. His prestige was growing, when an inquiry from President John A. Mackay asked whether we had a permanent post in view for Hromadka. When we replied in the negative, Princeton Seminary took him, and he served on its faculty very acceptably until the end of the War, when he felt he must return to his native land and help in the restoration of its Church. It has not often happened that Union has trained a professor for service in Princeton. However, Paul L. Lehmann, Union '30, Th.D. '36, has been on the faculty of Princeton Seminary since 1947.

During that appalling year when Hitler was overrunning his neighbors, we were appealed to by those who were caring for refugees from among the leaders of European Churches. One was a Polish Archbishop of the Orthodox Church, Archbishop Sava, whose diocese had been overrun by the Bolshevik forces. We provided this gentle soul with a room in the dormitory and placed Lampman Chapel at his disposal for his daily devotions; but he found them too solitary and asked whether we would admit him to our regular Chapel services. There he became a most faithful attender and commented often on how happily he became a sympathetic worshipper, and how fully he could enter into the hymns, prayers and even derive much inspiration from the brief addresses. Our students who came gradually to know him found him an interesting figure and an interpreter to them of a form of Christianity with which they were utterly unfamiliar. Hospitality to him revealed to us an angel whom we had not suspected. At one time almost an entire floor in the dormitory was taken by him and other persecuted Christians. Their presence brought the sufferings of the Churches of Europe vividly before the whole Seminary family.

## JOHN WESLEY WETZEL

In 1927 John Wesley Wetzel, a graduate of Southwestern College 1894 and of the Northwestern University School of Oratory, became Harkness Instructor in Public Speaking. He had taught in various seminaries and law schools, and was given a post at Columbia from 1921–28. Unhappily for Mr. Wetzel, his political and economic views clashed with those of many of the students, and when he tried to correct their aberrations they resented it. But he was an efficient expert in voice production and a good reader. A student was reading the familiar Christmas passage from St. Luke: "And they came with haste and found Mary, and Joseph, and the babe lying in a manger," and neglected to pause on the commas. Mr. Wetzel exclaimed "What a mangerful!" He was a painstaking interpreter of the Bible in his public reading. So discriminating a judge as Dr. Charles E. Jefferson invited him to be his associate at the Broadway Tabernacle in 1931, where he read the lesson every Sunday. He died in October 1945.

He was succeeded by the Rev. John Laurence Casteel, also a former student at Northwestern from which he received a Ph.D. in 1941. He had been Director of the Department of Speech at the University of Oregon and a frequent leader in student conferences. He proved a most satisfactory teacher, highly esteemed by Faculty and students. He was called away in 1951 to become Professor of Practical Theology at Colgate-Rochester Divinity School.

## WILLIAM M. KINGSLEY AND THATCHER BROWN

In 1936 William M. Kingsley felt compelled for reasons of health to lay down the Presidency of the Board of Directors. He had been a faithful administrator, always at the call of the President of the Faculty, invariably present at the meetings of the Board and of its Executive Committee, and familiar with the life of the Seminary. His humor, his friendliness, his sound judgment, his genuine piety, made him a valuable leader. His place was taken by Thatcher Magoun Brown, son and grandson of men who had served the Seminary for years. One of his grandfathers, Dr. William Adams, President of the Faculty 1873–1880, had been one of the founders in 1836 and an early Professor of Sacred Rhetoric; the other grandfather, James Brown, had been a benefactor of the institution who had set it on its feet financially by endowing professorships in the 1870's with a gift of $300,000. His father, John Crosby Brown, had been President of the Board 1898–1909, and Thatcher Brown had himself been a Director since 1908 and Treasurer of the Board 1923–36. Union Seminary was with him a heritage. He knew intimately its history and problems. He believed heartily in its purposes and was imbued with its spirit. A banker by profession, he gave much time and thought to the Seminary, came to all its important occasions, prepared carefully the very brief farewell words which he gave to graduating classes, and was available at all times for consultation with the President and other members of the Faculty. He was happily sympathetic with young men and their problems, and his broad and considerate leadership during the troubled days of student upsurgence in the 1930's and '40's was invaluable. He remained President until 1947 when he was succeeded by Benjamin Strong.

## ARTHUR JEFFERY

In 1937 President Nicholas Murray Butler of Columbia University was faced with a very difficult appointment. Dr. Gottheil who had held the Chair of Semitic Languages died, and there was a bitter rivalry among Zionists and anti-Zionists to fill the Chair. President Butler was advised to pass over both factions and appoint an Orientalist. The man suggested, however, proved a belligerent advocate of the Arabs, and both groups of Jews protested. Dr. Butler, accordingly, sent for the President of the Seminary and asked whether he knew a first-rate Orientalist. In 1935 he had become acquainted in the American University in Cairo with Dr. Arthur Jeffery, an Australian of remarkable scholarly ability, a graduate of the University of Melbourne, and of the Wesleyan College of Divinity in that city, who had taken both D.Phil. and D.Litt. degrees at Edinburgh and studied further in Germany and Paris, and gone out as Professor in Madras Christian College. When it was proposed after the missionary conference at Jerusalem in 1928 to establish a School of Oriental Studies for the preparation of men working in the Moslem world, he was taken to Cairo and placed in charge. The University of Leyden had asked him to edit a critical edition of the Koran. This would involve him in peril, for it would strike at the theory of the inerrancy of the Arabic text. Mrs. Jeffery was an American, so there was hope he might come to the United States. He accepted an invitation to lecture at Union, was most warmly received by the Columbia authorities and offered their Chair. As a devout Christian he much preferred some work in touch with future missionaries and ministers. It was therefore proposed that he should become Adjunct Professor at Union and be given an apartment among our Professors. For this he offered courses in History of Religions and in parts of the Old Testament, and became a loved and revered member of our Faculty, while discharging with distinction his work at Columbia. When *The Interpreter's Bible* was projected, he contributed to the first volume an essay on

"The Ancient Version and the text of the Old Testament."
Professor Jeffery soon became a sought-after figure in New
York pulpits.

## REINHOLD NIEBUHR

In the autumn of 1928 Reinhold Niebuhr, D.D., began
work at the Seminary as Associate Professor of Christian
Ethics. Born in 1892, educated at Elmhurst College, Eden
Theological Seminary and Yale Divinity School, he had been
pastor for thirteen years of the Bethel congregation of the
Evangelical Synod of North America in Detroit, and was
already a popular speaker at student conferences. He was
much interested in the relation of Christian theology to social
change, and soon after beginning his work at Union he dis-
tressed members of its Board of Directors by appearing as
a candidate for office on the Socialist ticket. The President
reassured them that on that ticket his chance of winning an
election was negligible. He was also a pacifist and had been
brought on to New York to assist in editing a pacifist paper.
Shortly his views changed and he became profoundly interested in theology, and developed his own variety of Neo-
Orthodoxy. This was a test of the genuineness and extent of
the Seminary's liberalism, for his views contravened those
taught at the time by Professors W. A. Brown and E. W.
Lyman, and were antagonistic to those of former President
McGiffert in which many of the alumni and Faculty had been
trained. Happily the liberalism of the Seminary was so stal-
wart that Niebuhr was listened to and after a short while became a most influential factor, not only at Union Seminary
but throughout the American Church. It is no exaggeration to

say that in the '30's and '40's he became a dominant force in Christian thinking throughout the universities and colleges of the country. An eloquent preacher, tirelessly going about to student congregations, a prolific writer, much less clear on the printed page than in moving speech, he was invited to lecture in Britain and on the Continent and became an international figure. He gave the Gifford Lectures in Edinburgh, where his audiences rivalled those who came to hear William James a generation before. These lectures were published under the title *The Nature and Destiny of Man* in two volumes in 1941 and 1942 and became at once a theological classic. He was appointed to the Dodge Chair of Applied Christianity in 1932 and was made Dean of the Faculty in 1950. For the past quarter-century, he has been a major force in shaping the thinking of Union students.

A former student writes:

Reinhold Niebuhr was a tremendous teacher. He was incapable of dullness in the classroom. Arriving a few minutes before class time, he stood at the lecturer's table like an eagle poised to swoop. His lecture notes furnished a well-organized development of thought, but they were only his taking-off place. From them he roved afield, seizing upon anything relevant to his theme. Everything, however ancient or minute, came alive and contemporary.

Niebuhr never concealed his own convictions. His style of teaching was highly personal. Whether one agreed or disagreed, he found Niebuhr stimulating. As his international reputation increased, both in religious and secular circles, his classes became more crowded, sometimes in the summer session straining the capacity of the Seminary's largest lecture hall. If a student group, planning a meeting, wanted to insure a large attendance, they tried to get, not a glamorous visiting speaker, but Niebuhr on the program.

No matter how many times he might have covered the same subject through the years, he approached it with the spontaneity of something new. I remember questioning him in class once, when he took the question with all the eagerness of a new and unsolved problem, went into it, and worked out an answer on the spot. I felt a real sense of accomplishment in having drawn him out. Then some weeks later I discovered that he had dealt with the same question in a book published years before. Yet there had been no false dramatics in his answer to me. His interest was not in the old problem but in the new personality raising it, and the spontaneity of his response was real.

Niebuhr's kindliness, known well to his students, was sometimes missed by those who from a distance saw only an awesome genius. He could in the same lecture be ferocious, biting, witty, thrilling. Yet he was always human—and Christian. Occasionally it happened that after a particularly scathing attack upon some viewpoint, some poor student would ask a question which showed that he not only had missed the whole point of Niebuhr's criticism but also that he represented the very position criticized. Then while the class waited with almost sadistic anticipation for Niebuhr to explode at the befuddled person, the teacher's attitude would relax as he patiently explained in the gentlest manner the point of his argument.

The energy and willingness of the man were boundless. It was not unusual for him to arrive at class with coat and suitcase, ready to leave hurriedly for the railroad station. I once caught him in mid-summer on a long week-end in New York between trips to Europe, the one trip for the church, the other for the State Department. He faced life with a great zest and, though it strained his health, found it hard to say "no."

With all the rush of his life, he made himself available to his students. He kept office hours faithfully, rarely accepted engagements which took him away from classes, and was always ready to consult with students. On several nights of each semester Mrs. Niebuhr and he were "at home" to students in their apartment. In a completely informal atmosphere with students crowding the chairs, window sills, and rugs of two rooms (with "Reinie" sitting between them), the conversation ranged far and wide. It might start with rolicking accounts of the Niebuhr children's adventures, move into the political arena (with Niebuhr telling of his conversations with high government officials), then get into theology. As a conversationalist, Reinie had the abilities of a virtuoso; but his conversations were never monologues and the most timid might find themselves drawn in. By noon of the next day the whole Seminary community might have heard "what went on up at the Niebuhrs last night."

## JOHN BAILLIE

In 1930 Professor William Adams Brown had been teaching Systematic Theology since his coming to the Seminary in 1890, and he asked that the Board relieve him of this task and appoint him Research Professor that he might have more leisure for writing and for his work in the Ecumenical Movement. His request was granted, and John Baillie, Professor of Systematic Theology in Emmanuel College, Toronto, was called to the Roosevelt Chair. Born in the Highlands of Scotland in 1886, educated at the University and New College, Edinburgh, with graduate work at Jena and Marburg, Baillie had been made Professor of Systematic Theology at Auburn in 1919. With eight years of teaching at Auburn and four at Toronto, Baillie came with experience and showed himself at once a clear and orderly lecturer, and a teacher who invited questions and answered them lucidly and frankly. He was a reinforcement to the Seminary as an eloquent and persuasive exponent of the historic heritage of the Church. He was sympathetic to the current scene but not dominated by it. He brought to contemporary problems the wealth of centuries of careful Christian thinking. He had published a number of volumes; and his lectures were so carefully written that they might readily be printed without much editing. His talks and prayers in Chapel were prepared with equal thoroughness and polish. He was a finished preacher. He battled valiantly with men whose presuppositions made them averse to the historic theology of the Church, and was beginning to have a commanding influence when, in 1934, he was called to the Professorship of Divinity in the University of Edinburgh. His departure was a great gain for Scotland and a sore impoverishment to the Seminary. The success of his work in Edinburgh and the high esteem in which he was held was witnessed by his election to the Moderatorship of the Church of Scotland in May 1943 and to the Principalship of New College in 1951.

A student who worked under Baillie, writes of him:

One of the really great things he did in his four years at Union was to play a large part in giving purposeful direction to the upswing of interest in doctrinal theology, after the doldrums it had fallen into in the '20's.

An alumnus, who after several very fruitful pastorates is now a Professor of Practical Theology, writes:

The greatest thing about Baillie was that he always addressed his powerful mind to the great issues of Christian thought and experience. And he brought his students to do the same. No one could accuse him of dealing with marginal issues, and no one who sat under his lectures or did his assigned reading could fail to come to terms with the elementary verities of Christian faith or grapple with the fundamental questions of life. God, Man, Sin, Salvation, the Meaning of Jesus Christ, Immortality—these were the great themes of his thinking. He had a certain genius in understanding the temper and talking the language of the skeptic or worldling. But he was never maneuvered into being a mere defender of the faith. Christianity, in the last analysis, for him was not a Problem, although it involved problems; it was the Answer, and he gave it boldly and profoundly.

The next thing that impressed me was his incisive, relentless logic. There was something inescapable about his thinking. Once you started with him, you could not stop. It was not that he intellectually tyrannized over his students; on the contrary, he was eminently fair-minded and patient. It was rather that he moved straight down the central path of thought in whatever subject he was dealing with, and the student could not help being carried along. For this reason, incidentally, it was always easy to take notes on Baillie's lectures. They were so well organized that they practically wrote themselves down on paper.

But beneath the depth and clarity of his thought there always beat the undertones of his own devotion. One does not forget his quiet prayers at the opening of class, nor the reverence with which he dealt with great themes of theology. While his lectures were rigorously intellectual, they were never merely that; one felt that they were the fruit of prayer and faith as well.

I am not sure that Baillie could be described as a "popular" lecturer. In my seminary years systematic theology was somewhat crowded out by more fashionable but more superficial disciplines, e.g. religious education. And many students did not realize that we had a very great man among us. Some students also found him unapproachable. This, I think, was due to a certain native shyness. But those who sought him out in friendship found him ever eager to be a friend, and socially he was the most delightful of companions. I will always cherish the memory of a most rich friendship both in the classroom and outside it.

## HARRISON ELLIOTT

With the sudden resignation of Professor George Albert Coe in the summer of 1922, the Seminary had to seek someone to head the work in Religious Education. It chose as Assistant Professor, Harrison Sackett Elliott, B.A. Ohio Wesleyan, and B.D. from Drew Theological Seminary, with an M.A. at Columbia University. Mr. Elliott had considerable experience in practical work both in the Methodist Church and the Y. M. C. A. He had been a secretary under the International Committee of the latter organization, and had served as instructor in Drew as well as teaching in the Training School of the Y. W. C. A. He began his work at Union at a time when Religious Education was a very popular subject. As a student of Professor Dewey, Professor Kilpatrick and Professor Coe, he adopted their educational views. He was a leading exponent of the discussion method. In 1923 the Association Press brought out his *The Why and How of Group Discussion.* In 1928 he developed the subject further in *The Process of Group Thinking,* and in 1946 he returned to the theme in *Group Discussion in Religious Education.* He was full of vital energy and gave himself unstintedly to his students. He was always ready to receive their confidence and listen to their problems. The amount of time he lavished on interviews was prodigious. Many a man is most grateful for this personal counsel. He was a militant advocate of his educational theories, and ready to explain and defend them against all comers. In the 1920's he made these views apparently dominant in the thinking of a majority of students. One recalls a brash youth saying publicly at a Retreat: "The Scotch and other uneducated professors." It was a condemnation of all who taught without employing the prized method of group discussion. But it was a superficial and most unintelligent verdict on Professors Black, Ross, and Scott, and on many of their American-born colleagues. After the 1920's the Seminary settled to a saner and more inclusive view of educational methods. Towards the close of his teaching career Professor Elliott himself came to employ lectures much more often. In the 1930's a violent controversy over religious education broke out with books by professors in various institutions. Professor Elliott voiced his convictions in a trenchant volume: *Can Religious Education be Christian?*" On his retirement he was called to become the executive of the Religious Education Association, but his health was poor and he died suddenly in the summer of 1950.

One of his students has written concerning him:

As I recall my own student days during Dr. Elliott's first years here, I feel that students were intrigued and stimulated by his genuine faith in the values which would come from group thinking and from individual student participation in the work of his classes. We came to realize that he meant what he said when he urged us to do our own thinking and to come to conclusions by a group process in which issues were fairly faced and every person shared in the quest for the truth. In the early days there was frustration and irritation because he would not lecture to us, as some of us wished, mixed with a growing sense of appreciation of what his principles of individual development really meant. He kept pushing us to discover the divinely or-

dained processes by which we and others could grow, insisted
that there were certain conditions to be met if Christian education were to be effective, and trusted us as individual students
to make discoveries which would be genuinely creative. It was
his faith in inherent personal values and capacities which was
responsible, I believe, for the deep loyalty which many students
developed towards him. As I say, some were repelled and went
to other professors who would present material in more formal
fashion and give them the lectures which they wished. But his
loyal following was based finally not upon curiosity about his
methods, but on appreciation of them and a sense of their fundamental value.

Another student, now a professor, writes of him:

In the classroom Professor Elliott demonstrated his reliance
upon the process of group thinking as a means of helping students discover possibilities in themselves which they may or
may not have previously realized. Education as progressive
growth of the whole person, rather than a mere matter of the
mind encompassing information, certainly had meaning for me
when Professor Elliott conducted his classes. His unfailing respect for any man's idea, plus his insistence on a functional Christianity, were contributions I received from him. As a teacher he
was exceeded by himself as a man. I was grateful for his guidance
and his friendship.

When Elliott married Miss Grace Loucks, the brilliant and
devoted Secretary of the Y. W. C. A., he did me (H. S. C.)
the honor to ask me to officiate at the ceremony. I arrived
from the sleeper early one morning and he met me to drive
me some twenty miles to the Loucks home. I remarked that
I had been trying to see where the group participated in the
marriage ceremony, and could think only of the point where

the question is asked whether any here present knows any just reason why they should not be united in marriage. To which after a pause Elliott remarked, "I think we can leave the group out."

Another graduate writes of Professor Elliott:

In his courses students experienced the democratic method in group work. Skillful in the discussion method, which he employed almost exclusively in his classes, they witnessed in him the actual practice of the techniques of non-directive leadership. While a single period seemed diffuse, a year's work in the course would cover the major areas of the educational task of the Church, with emphasis upon the practical techniques of applying the democratic method.

## JAMES MOFFATT

It had been hoped that when Dr. McGiffert was relieved of administrative duties as President of the Faculty, he might be able to give at least one course a semester. But his health continued to be miserable, and it was evident that the Washburn Chair must be filled. The choice fell on the Rev. Professor James Moffatt, D.D., D.Litt., a renowned Biblical scholar, then occupying the history chair in the United Free Church College, Glasgow. Born in 1870, educated at Glasgow University, he had served in two charges in the United Free Church, at Dundonald and Broughty Ferry, then had been Yates Professor of Greek at Mansfield College, Oxford (1911–15), and had taken the history chair in Glasgow. He had published many books, especially the *Introduction to the New Testament*, had given the commentary to two books in the *Expositor's Greek Testament*, and was known internationally for his translation of the Bible. A man of charming personality, enormously learned, an omnivorous reader, he brought a famous reputation to the Seminary. When he was invited to deliver a series of lectures at Duke University in Durham, North Carolina, a colleague passing through neighboring Raleigh, the railway center, saw a headline in the morning newspaper AUTHOR OF BIBLE TO LECTURE AT DUKE. This was clipped and put up on the Seminary bulletin board with the comment: "We had not known the eminence of Union's new professor." His vast erudition, which he carried most modestly, made it difficult for him to finish any course which he undertook. One of these entitled *The Great Sequence* supposedly covered Church History from the second through the sixth centuries, but rarely completed the third. Students joked of it as "The Great Sequence which stopped seeking." He had written a delightful small volume on George Meredith and gave courses in Dante. No man on the Faculty was more widely familiar with literature, as his literary illustrations to Biblical passages attest. He had a humor which debunked presumptuous piety. The adherents of Frank N. D. Buchman invaded New York and invited our Scots professors to a lunch at the University Club, where there was much "sharing." On his return, Moffatt commented: "They reverse the New Testament: let your *sins* so shine before men!" It was he who suggested the motto over the entrance of the Refectory: *Cognoverunt eum in fractione panis.*

While working steadily on lectures and in counselling numbers of students on their theses, he found time to edit various commentaries and to publish a volume of his own almost every year. He was indefatigable. Probably he wrote too much, for some of his books lack the charm and substance of others; but the total output of his unresting pen is impressive. At times he had a genius for titles, as his *The Thrill of Tradition,* which gave his point at once. He never took any exercise, and his one diversion was to watch professional baseball on which he became an authority, knowing the names, batting averages, and particular skills of numbers of players. During Summer Sessions he often went with parties of ministers to the Polo Grounds and the management furnished him a complimentary season ticket. He had a weak voice which made his preaching in large churches difficult to hear, but his talks at morning Chapel were always rich in spiritual content and in illustrations. He became Professor-emeritus in 1938 but continued as Secretary of the Committee preparing the Revised Standard Version of the Bible, and worked as unweariedly as ever until death overtook him on June 27, 1944.

One of his most brilliant students writes of him:

He was one of the most learned men on the faculty. The range of his reading and knowledge was enormous. He could have filled almost any chair in the older disciplines. He was historian, critic, theologian, linguist and litterateur. Known chiefly for his renowned translation of the Bible, he wrote on Biblical topics, Church history, literature and the devotional life, and even indulged in a pseudonymous detective story.

His lectures evidenced his wide learning without parading it. They were written in a sharp and pointed style, and were pronounced with a Scottish accent which was sometimes the despair of the Junior. He was interested in detail, in human and colorful incidents, and especially in biography. He had a warm sympathy and a rich imagination, and his lectures, like his sermons, often betrayed his experience as a pastor. He had a certain native wisdom which, combined with the gentleness of his personality, gave him great charm as a teacher. While he was seldom electric in the classroom, he was always fresh and perceptive.

Another, for whom Moffatt had so high a regard that he asked him to write one of the commentaries he was then editing, says of him:

His lectures were formal, well balanced, informative, but not inspiring. I really never got to know him, though I did one of the volumes in his series; he had so much Scotch reserve. His uncommunicativeness was more properly perhaps my inability to communicate with him. It led me to fail to use in my commentary on Mark a new edition of his translation which I did not know he had completed. It annoyed him no end; but he made all the necessary changes himself and never bothered me about it. I only learned it after the episode was over.

## RUSSELL BOWIE

In 1926 Walter Russell Bowie came on the Faculty as a Lecturer on Homiletics. Born in Richmond, Virginia, in 1882, a graduate of Harvard and of the Episcopal Theological Seminary in Alexandria, which had permitted him to take his senior year at Union with the Class of 1908, Bowie served as rector at Greenwood, Virginia (1908–11), of St. Paul's in Richmond (1911–23), with a term as chaplain in World War I, then as rector of Grace Church, New York City, 1923–39. He had a flair for literature and, besides several volumes of sermons, he published a number of books of popular Bible exposition, *The Master*, 1928; and again *The Story of Jesus*, 1937; *Great Men of the Bible*, 1934; *The Story of the Bible*, 1937; he became Associate Editor of *The Interpreter's Bible*, writing the exposition of *Genesis,* and of the first part of *Luke,* and an article on the *Parables.* With imagination he made Biblical scenes and incidents vivid, and was particularly successful in preaching to boys and girls. A number of his children's sermons were published. He served with the New Testament Committee on the Revised Standard Version, and helped polish the English. Students at Union found him very sympathetic and helpful. He was a member of the Board of Directors, 1923–39. His voice was ineffective in a building as large as Grace Church and militated against his popularity as a preacher, but in the classroom it was no hindrance to him. In 1939 he was called to fill the Jesup Chair of Practical Theology and his Biblical expositions were highly prized for their suggestiveness, their poetic quality and their insight into the Biblical books. His hymns, of which a number are in hymnals, and his prayers, *Lift Up Your Hearts,* are a notable contribution to the worship of the Church. In 1945 he became Dean of Students, where his personal friendship with students endeared him to many. On his retirement in 1950 he was called to the Homiletics Chair in the Episcopal Seminary at Alexandria.

A man of vast versatility with a subtle humor and poetic gifts, a thorough scholar, Bowie added much in culture, in devoutness, in civic spirit to the life of the Seminary. A former student, commenting on his skill in the Homiletic Class, tells of a student's sermon which was rather dull but in which there was a metaphor. Bowie criticized the sermon with sympathy and gentleness, and then, taking up the metaphor, praised it, and said "Let me show you what you missed." Out of the metaphor, with singular felicity of language he developed an entire sermon that appealed to the class as most effective and beautiful. The student who was speaking of Bowie concluded by remarking that he taught them that no sermon was really written until it was written beautifully. Mrs. Bowie, who suffered a seriously crippling illness while they were at Union, made a deep impression on the whole Seminary by her gallantry, her humor, her penetrating comments on public men and events, and drew to their apartment a constant series of visitors, older and younger. When they left for Alexandria she, as well as her husband, was sorely missed.

## BUSINESS ADMINISTRATION

In 1923 Charles Trumbull White, son of Professor Gaylord S. White, a graduate of Princeton University with several years experience in banking, was appointed Bursar by the Board of Directors. He proved a useful and efficient manager of the Seminary's financial affairs. He found an office which was somewhat confused and where the personal qualities of his predecessor had developed ill-will from both Faculty and students. Mr. White brought a new orderliness in the management, and addressed himself with skill to the plans for the enlargement of the Seminary's equipment in the Brown Memorial Tower, the Refectory and Social Hall, and the new dormitory, McGiffert Hall. His unremitting attention saved the Seminary many dollars and enabled the plans to be conformed to the desires of those who were to occupy and use the new quarters. He was of utmost assistance to the new President who assumed office in 1926 and took many details of administration from his hands. During his service restless students were constantly proposing and pushing plans for the organization of the staff in line with more radical social and industrial arrangements. Mr. White dealt patiently with them and kept the business affairs of the institution moving smoothly. The Directors recognized his services and promoted him to be Comptroller, with added responsibilities for the portfolio of investments. This post he filled until 1950 when he was asked by the United States Government to take a position in its administration in the Near East. His family had long been associated with the Seminary so that it was an hereditary interest with him, and his own loyalty and fidelity to its affairs form a bright chapter in its recent history.

Over the years Union Seminary has been most fortunate in employees who have served for long periods and become endeared to students and members of the Faculty. Mr. Emanuel Romero, who began his service when the Seminary still stood at 700 Park Avenue, came up to the new site and ever since has been in charge of the office in Hastings Hall, the men's dormitory. At this writing he has been on the staff more than forty-five years and successive classes of students know him well and hold him in respect and affection. Mr. James Anderson has been in charge of the General Office since 1910, has seen many of the Faculty come and go, and has had part in the various official events in the Seminary's history. Mr. George Bayley has also been with the institution since 1910, for years in charge of the grounds, more recently at the telephone switchboard in Knox Hall. Mr. Charles Henry has served since 1913. These long-time helpers feel that the Seminary is their charge and they have done much by their devotion to set the tone and spirit in which the entire working staff fulfils its tasks.

CHAPTER VIII

# AUBURN AND UNION JOIN

In the spring of 1939 representatives of Auburn Theological Seminary approached Union with a view to arranging an association of the two Seminaries in New York City. Auburn had been established in 1818 by a group of ministers and laymen profoundly concerned with providing the Gospel for the growing population towards the West. They were Presbyterians and Congregationalists, for in western New York many of the congregations were unions of the two. The Presbyterian General Assembly of 1801 had authorized such combinations, and there was a feeling that a training school for ministers was sorely needed to supply leaders in this section of the country. The proponents of the institution had applied for aid to the General Assembly, but the Assembly was occupied in maintaining the seminary which had been founded at Princeton. Accordingly a number of presbyteries in the Synod of Geneva (later New York) went forward with their plan, and located their seminary at Auburn as a convenient center for the towns and villages of that rapidly increasing section. These founders, like those of Union, were men of broad mind, already familiar with co-operation in the life and work of the Church. In their Charter is a proviso:

that no student of any Christian denomination shall be excluded from a participation in the privileges of this institution on the ground of his religious persuasion.

One of the founders of Union, Dr. Samuel Hanson Cox, had served as a professor at Auburn, and down through the years the men of Auburn and the men of Union had found themselves often shoulder to shoulder in the conflicts within the Presbyterian Church. Several of the members of the Union Faculty, notably Dr. W. G. T. Shedd, had served on the Auburn Faculty, and Dr. George William Knox was a graduate of Auburn. In the struggles with Fundamentalism the liberals had drawn up a statement of their principles in 1926 in reply to the attempt to alter the historic vow in the ordination of ministers and other office-bearers by setting forth five interpretations as "essential and necessary." This statement was drafted by a group who met in the Brick Presbyterian Church in New York City, but it was printed and published at Auburn and became known as "The Auburn Affirmation." Both Auburn and Union had been linked with the New School wing of the Church after the disruption of 1837–38, and the alumni of the two seminaries found themselves of similar theological and ecclesiastical mind.

Social changes during the nineteenth century had drawn students to seminaries in great cities and associated with universities. Auburn's student body, which in the mid-century was as numerous as Union's, had shrunk to diminutive proportions, and its resources were inadequate for the maintenance of a first-rate academic institution. Attempts had been made under the vigorous leadership of President George B. Stewart, and later under President Paul S. Heath, to move the seminary to a more metropolitan site. A committee of the General Assembly had advised its combination with Colgate-Rochester, a Baptist seminary, at Rochester. The effort, however, to raise the money required to erect new buildings at the Rochester site had failed of its goal. The plan now proposed involved no additional funds, but the location of the seminary at the Union site, and the continuation of both seminaries in partnership. Several of the Auburn Faculty had retired or were on the point of retiring; President Heath was about to accept a pastorate, and only two professors were available for work under the new arrangement. The plan safeguarded the continuance of both Boards of Directors, the maintenance of existing financial controls, and allowed the partnership in service to grow gradually and settle just what particular task should be assigned to each seminary.

There was opposition to the plan on the part of a few in the Auburn constituency and of some in the leadership of the Presbyterian Church. A lawsuit to prevent the proposed association was begun. The Court, however, disposed of the objections rapidly in view of the counsel for the General Assembly which had favored the earlier project of affiliation with a Baptist institution and of the freedom granted to Auburn under its Charter. The legal advisers of the Union Directors saw no difficulty in the fact that the Auburn Directors were elected by seventeen presbyteries inasmuch as each institution maintained its chartered existence and financial integrity. After the association began to operate in the autumn of 1939, the President of the Union Faculty was elected to a corresponding position in Auburn and made a member of its Board of Directors. Several members of the Auburn Board were elected to fill vacancies in Union's Board. The two Professors, Dr. Robert Hastings Nichols and the

Rev. Walter Seaman Davison, were elected Professors of Church History and Practical Theology respectively in Union. After some negotiations, Auburn resumed an earlier practice of reporting annually to the Presbyterian General Assembly. Its scholarship funds were used for the assistance of Presbyterian students. Its library was combined with that of Union, and it took over the circulating theological library for alumni which had been set up at Union in 1928. It has conducted conferences for ministers both in New York City, and in various presbyteries throughout the State of New York. In 1952 its directors erected Auburn Hall, a very beautiful and useful building on the south end of the Union quadrangle. The years from 1939 have been a happy partnership without friction.

The President of the Auburn Board of Directors, Henry Hamlin Stebbins, Jr., son of a graduate of Union in 1867, was a most helpful factor in all the negotiations and in the first years of the association of the two seminaries. His death in the summer of 1952 was a sore loss to both Boards.

A graduate who was a student at Union at the time of the merger writes of Professor Nichols:

He was respected as a fine scholar and a splendid teacher. His course in American Church History was well received and he was recognized as one of the great authorities in that field of study. He taught a seminar on the Creeds of Christendom, and students agreed that it was the most helpful course taught on the meaning of the Protestant faith. He was a tireless champion of the liberal tradition, his faith firmly rooted in the best of Calvinism, with a friendly interest in each of his students.

This man, an honored pastor in the Middle West, told me that he had acquired his working theology as a preacher from Professor Nichols and could never be sufficiently grateful to him. His testimony can easily be multiplied.

Of Dean Walter S. Davison, one writes:

He not only knew his students while they were at Union, but ten years later could call them by name. His personal interest has helped many a student in the interpretation of Scripture, in prayer and in the devotional life. He has been beloved as teacher, counsellor and friend.

Both Auburn Professors made their places at once and captured the honor and affection of their classes. Professor Nichols retired in 1944 and was succeeded by Professor John T. McNeill, who was called to Union from the Divinity Faculty of the University of Chicago where he held the Chair of the History of European Christianity. Professor Davison remained in active service until 1953, and another graduate of Auburn, the Rev. Charles Erwin Mathews, took over his work and became Dean of Auburn.

# CHAPTER IX

# THE SCHOOL OF SACRED MUSIC

SHORTLY after Dr. Coffin's assumption of the Presidency, Dr. and Mrs. Clarence Dickinson talked with him of a project they had in their minds as a dream for the future—a School of Sacred Music at Union Seminary, training men and women as choir-directors and organists. The new President had already been thinking of such a development, and their project at once met a sympathetic response. New York City was the musical center of the world. One could easily procure here the best teachers, and without too much difficulty collect a distinguished faculty. It would be a great advantage to have future choir-directors educated side by side with ministers: they would understand public worship and imbibe the outlook of the Church, and in turn they would enhance the aesthetic appreciation of ministers. Such a school would involve little immediate expense for equipment—perhaps some additional organs for practice, an increase in the musical library, some scholarship aid, and so forth. The President talked the subject over with one or two of the Directors whom he hoped to interest and found them favorably disposed.

The Seminary had always provided some instruction in music for its ministerial students. As early as 1837 Abner Jones had been appointed Instructor in Sacred Music. Among his successors were several who had left names in American music—George Frederick Root, composer of a few tunes for hymns and of such well-known songs as "There's Music in the Air," "The Battle-cry of Freedom," "Tramp, Tramp, Tramp, the Boys are Marching"; above all Lowell Mason, editor of several collections of hymns and anthems, and the composer of many favorite tunes. One of his associates in training choirs had been Thomas Hastings, also a composer of a number of favorite tunes, and the father of a future President of the Seminary. The Harkness Instructorship in Music had been endowed in the 1880's, and was held for twenty-two years by Gerrit Smith, Mus.Doc., a founder of the American Guild of Organists who gave the Guild its name and became its first warden. In 1912 he was succeeded in the Instructorship in Music by Clarence Dickinson. He had been the arranger of many carols, anthems, etc., and the composer of a number in wide use in the churches. In addition to his teaching, Dr. Dickinson gave historical lectures on sacred music for the general public.

The subject of the establishment of such a School of Sacred Music was brought up at the Board of Directors on January 10, 1928 and given a full discussion. No opposition was encountered but misgivings were expressed as to cost and a possible drain on the Seminary's funds. The President then took the matter to two of the generous friends of the Seminary, and received from them pledges which enabled us to go ahead with definite plans. Dr. and Mrs. Dickinson laid out a curriculum, approached several noted musicians, and were ready to issue an announcement to would-be students. We applied to the Regents of the University of the State of New York for permission to offer the Master's degree in Sacred Music to students who entered with a Bachelor's degree, whether in Arts or Science or Music. A requirement of previous musical training was laid down. The curriculum also provided that students should take not less than ten points in the courses offered to theological students. This would enable them to be efficient helpers in the work of Sunday Schools and young people's societies, and give them a background in the Bible, Church history or theology. In fact, several of those who had taken the course in sacred music have returned to complete the whole course in theology and are serving as pastors of churches.

The School opened in the autumn of 1928, with an enrollment of twenty-six candidates for the degree and twenty part-time students. It became at once apparent that a fresh stimulus had been brought into the Seminary's life. The choir which led our chapel services was reinforced, informal music was furnished in the Social Room, and theological students began to have an intelligent interest in the musical happenings in the city. Dr. Dickinson directed a lovely service of carols at Christmas-time, arranged for two oratorios each year which the music students conducted and accompanied on the organ, and in the late spring scheduled an evening of original organ compositions and anthems by students in the school. We had no difficulty in placing the graduates, and had many more applications than could be accepted. Posts in colleges and schools, as well as in churches, sought musicians.

The students in this school were different in type of mind from the candidates in theology—on the whole more devout and less critical, more conservative in accepting and revering existing institutions in Church and society, and less given to radical agitation. Thus they helped to balance the Seminary's interests.

Changes have been made in the physical arrangements for the School. In 1941 Arthur Curtiss James, just before his death, generously provided for the rebuilding and enlargement of the organ in the Chapel—a gift whose result he did not live to enjoy, but for which congregations who worship daily and on Sundays bless his memory. In 1953 the tower of the James Chapel has been fitted up with rooms in which musical students may practice playing or singing without disturbing others in the Seminary community. Although the School is still young, it has acquired a reputation throughout the country, and several of its graduates have attained posts of distinction. It became evident after a few years that some of them would wish further study, and the Regents in 1941 granted permission to confer the degree of Doctor of Sacred Music. In the years immediately following, this degree was won by thirty-four men and women.

At the centennial of the Seminary in 1936, and again in recognition of the retirement of Dr. and Mrs. Dickinson in 1945, the School called in its alumni at work in the New York area with their choirs, and gave services of choral music under Dr. Dickinson's leadership in the Riverside Church. These were striking evidence of the contribution made in a short time to the musical life of the churches.

In 1952–53, on the occasion of the Twenty-fifth Anniversary of the founding of the School of Sacred Music, the graduates of the School throughout the world joined in celebration of its first quarter century. Over one hundred concerts, recitals and services of recognition were held in cities and churches in all parts of this country, and, indeed, in several lands overseas. The celebration culminated in a Festival of Sacred Music in the Riverside Church on the evening of May fifth, when some twenty-five choirs trained by alumni or students of the School were led by Dr. Porter and Dr. Dickinson in a program which occasioned much favorable comment.

## CLARENCE AND HELEN DICKINSON

The Seminary was fortunate to possess in these devout and devoted Christians, outstanding figures both in the Church and in the realm of music, leaders to mould and direct this new School in its formative years. Dr. Clarence Dickinson, B.A. of Northwestern in 1894 and M.A. in 1909, had pursued his musical studies in Berlin and in Paris, had held posts as organist and choirmaster in churches and synagogues in Chicago and New York, and was nationally known. Northwestern and Ohio Wesleyan Universities had recognized his eminence with the degree of Doctor of Music, and Miami University had conferred upon him its degree of Doctor of Letters. He combined lofty standards of musical taste with an unerring sense of the music helpful to a worshipping congregation, skillful musicianship with a reverent spirit, loyalty to the tradition of the Church throughout the centuries with a willingness to explore with sympathy the innovators attempting new forms today.

Dr. Helen Adell Dickinson, an M.A. of Queen's University at Kingston, Ontario and a Ph.D. in 1901 at Heidelberg University, Germany, lectured on the Historic Liturgies and their Music, and on Religious Art. She and her husband worked together on all his recitals and public lectures—a unique couple, complementing each other and together communicating to their students their conviction of music as an essential ministry of the Christian Church. Dr. Clarence Dickinson was chosen Editor of the *Hymnal,* issued in 1933 by the Presbyterian Church and used widely beyond the bounds of that Communion. He is loved and revered by the students of the Seminary as a great Christian. The services which he has arranged in the Chapel to illustrate the usages in worship in the Church and the Synagogue have familiarized future ministers and choirmasters with the wealth available in the various traditions of God's people.

Dr. Dickinson was succeeded as Director of the School in 1945 by Hugh Porter, a graduate of the School in its first class (1930) who had received the doctorate in 1944. His Chair now bears the name of the Clarence and Helen Dickinson Professorship of Sacred Music.

## THE MUSIC SCHOOL FACULTY

One of the first to receive the degree in Sacred Music characterizes other members of the Faculty:

Dr. Frederick Schlieder, teacher of organ, composition, and theory, is known chiefly for his methods of teaching improvisation, which he has set forth in several text books on the subject. Probably the best known of these is *Lyric Composition through Improvisation.* He taught improvisation at the School of Sacred Music from the time of its founding until his death in 1952. In presenting the subject he covered all forms of theory and composition from the simplest harmonic patterns of a few measures in length to the elaborate homophonic and polyphonic forms for piano and organ.

Dr. Miles Farrow, master of the choir of The Cathedral of St. John the Divine, instituted the course in Boy Choir Training and Anglican Chanting in the School of Sacred Music. Every few weeks it was his custom to bring to the Seminary a group of choir boys from the Cathedral dressed in navy blue and wearing Buster Brown collars who vocalized for the class, illustrated principles of good chanting and sang anthems from their repertory. On Dr. Farrow's retirement this course was carried on in good English tradition by Dr. T. Tertius Noble and later by Dr. Norman Coke-Jephcott, master of the choir and organist of The Cathedral of St. John the Divine.

Dr. T. Tertius Noble, for fifteen years the organist and choirmaster of York Minister Cathedral in England, resigned that position in 1913 to accept a similar post at St. Thomas' Church, New York City. There he played the organ and directed the choir of men and boys until his retirement in 1945. From 1932 until 1947 he taught the course in Boy Choir Training and from 1941 to 1947 he was in charge of the teaching of composition and instrumentation. Dr. Noble's compositions include anthems, cantatas, chorale preludes and many large works for the organ. He also has to his credit chamber and orchestral works.

Dr. Edwin J. Stringham, composer and educator, scholarship student at the Royal Academy in Rome in 1929, Cromwell Traveling Fellow in Germany in 1936, author of a number of books on acoustics and theory, taught composition at the School of Sacred Music from the time of its founding until 1939 when he resigned to become Chairman of the Department of Music at Queens College, N. Y. C. In his teaching Dr. Stringham had unusual ability to stimulate the imagination and creative bent of his students. At the end of each year members of his class of candidates for the master's degree gave a concert of original compositions in James Chapel. Choral and orchestral compositions of Dr.

Stringham have been performed by major symphony orchestras throughout the country.

For twenty-four years Mrs. William Neidlinger, director of the St. Cecilia Choir of St. Michael's Church, New York, taught vocal art, phonetics, and diction in the School of Sacred Music. Both organ and voice students profited by her intense interest in voice and her love for teaching. Besides her class work she gave private lessons in voice. She gave her time and energy without stint. Many a student received extra hours of coaching in her studio at St. Michael's Church in addition to the help she had given them in the regular classes at the Seminary.

The course in Plainsong was instituted by Canon Charles Winfred Douglas whose vigorous and varied career as lecturer, author, musicologist, liturgiologist and pastor had made him known in every field of church music in America. He was musical editor of *The New Hymnal* (Episcopal), 1916, and of *The Hymnal* (Episcopal), 1940; co-editor with Wallace Goodrich of *The Choral Service;* author of *Church Music in History and Practice* and editor of *The American Missal.* The tune "St. Dunstan's" which he composed for Bunyan's words, "He Who Would Valiant Be" is one of the strongest and finest of recent hymn tunes.

Canon Douglas was followed by Harold Beckett Gibbs, devotee of and instructor in Plainsong and Polyphonic Music, 1928–1945. Born in England in 1868 he had served as organist in a number of Anglo-Catholic and Roman Catholic Churches in Britain and in this country. He was a recognized authority in his subject, and made it appealing to those whom he taught. A very devout Christian, he joined in the worship of the Chapel, although a Roman Catholic, and he and his wife entered fully into the Seminary life. While teaching in Union he was organist and·choirmaster of St. Ignatius Episcopal Church.

From 1928 to 1946 Franklin W. Robinson lectured at the

School of Sacred Music on Aural Harmony and the Philosophy
of Music. It was not his purpose to teach music theory in the
conventional way but to bring the student to a realization of
the fundamental nature of music by a study of keys and chords
as emotional symbols. He believed that their use and relationship in great music expressed fundamental spiritual and emotional values. Mr. Robinson also taught at the Institute of Musical Art and at the Juilliard Graduate School. He was one of
the founders of the National Orchestral Association.

## MUSIC SCHOOL ALUMNI

In this connection we may speak of some of Union's
alumni who have contributed to the hymnody of the Church.

The first is George Duffield, 1840, the author of "Stand Up,
Stand Up for Jesus"—a hymn written in 1858 for Sunday
School children which attained popularity among the soldiers
on both sides of the conflict in the Civil War, and is in widespread use in both the United States and Great Britain and
throughout the English-speaking world. Duffield also wrote
other hymns but none so well known.

A second is Edward Hopper, 1842, who, while minister
of the Church of the Sea and Land at Market and Henry
Streets in New York, wrote "Jesus, Saviour Pilot Me," which
was set to music by John E. Gould, and has passed into wide
use in the United States and Canada.

Another is Aaron Roberts Wolfe, 1851, who wrote a concluding hymn for a service of Holy Communion—"A Parting
Hymn We Sing." It is in fairly widespread use in Presbyterian and similar churches in the U. S. A.

William Pierson Merrill, 1890, for many years minister of
the Brick Presbyterian Church in New York, has contributed

both hymns and tunes. Of the former, his "Rise Up, O Men of God," 1911, is in most current hymnals in many communions, both in Great Britain and the United States. Some Anglican editors have omitted verse three because it speaks of the Church's strength as "unequal to her task," but the latest Protestant Episcopal hymnal in this country includes it. A fine national hymn, written the same year, "Not Alone for Might and Empire" has been set to a singable Welsh tune "Hyfrydol," and has an increasing vogue. Merrill is also a musician. His tunes *America Befriend,* written for words by one of his predecessors, Henry van Dyke; *Marcus Whitman,* a setting for a fine National Missions hymn by Robert Freeman, as well as an earlier tune, composed in 1885 for "Soldiers of Christ, Arise" are in the 1933 edition of *The Hymnal* of the Presbyterian Church U. S. A., and in other collections.

Henry Hallam Tweedy, 1896, minister in various churches and Professor in the Yale Divinity School, has written a number of hymns and been the editor of a hymnal, *Christian Worship and Praise,* 1939. Of his hymns, the best known is perhaps "O Gracious Father of Mankind," which won the prize in a hymn contest held in 1925. Harry Emerson Fosdick, 1904, in addition to his many talents, possesses the poetic gift. "God of Grace and God of Glory" written for the dedication of the Riverside Church, has been widely used. "O God in Restless Living," written in 1931, and a hymn for international peace, "The Prince of Peace His Banner Spreads," have come into use in a number of the churches.

Walter Russell Bowie, 1908, rector of St. Paul's, Richmond, and of Grace Church, New York City, Professor of Practical Theology both at Union and later at the Virginia Theological Seminary in Alexandria, has written a number of hymns of high lyric merit. "O Holy City, Seen of John," 1909, is in wide use. A hymn on the nation, "God of the Nations, Who from Dawn of Days," has been included in several collections, as has "Lord, Through Changing Days, Unchanging." Still another on the social embodiment of the Gospel, "Lovely to the Outward Eye," has decided merit.

James Gordon Gilkey, 1915, has contributed a Palm Sunday hymn, "Outside the Holy City," which is in at least one collection.

The story of Sacred Music in the life of Union Seminary, not only during the first quarter century of the School of Sacred Music but also during the almost ninety years which preceded its founding, is charmingly set forth by one of the recent graduates of the School, Miss Ellouise H. Skinner, in a small booklet published in connection with the Twenty-fifth Anniversary celebrations in 1953, *Sacred Music in Union Theological Seminary, 1836–1953: An Informal History.*

# CHAPTER X

# CHANGING STUDENT CONCERNS

DURING the half century in which we are tracing the history of Union Seminary, the theological climate underwent a number of changes; and these affected both its curriculum and its life. Throughout the late 1880's and the '90's, interest was focused on the Old Testament. The application of the methods of historical criticism to its books was the cause of current ecclesiastical conflicts. Students offered few objections to the requirement of Hebrew. They wished to be capable of distinguishing the Jahvist from the Elohist narratives, and some knowledge of the original language was obviously indispensable. Every Junior began his course with six required hours per week in Hebrew Grammar, and in exercises in translating Hebrew into English and English into Hebrew. Brighter and more industrious men, if they took university courses to supplement those given in the Seminary, usually took them in the Oriental languages.

We all knew Greek, for the classics were a staple in liberal arts colleges, and in those days college entrants were examined in both elementary Latin and Greek. Seminary Juniors as a rule had had from three to six years' study in Greek. Before the exploration of the *koine*, it was assumed that the Greek of the New Testament had been providentially designed as a vehicle for the Christian revelation. Pagan terms could not contain and communicate the spiritual wealth of the Gospel, so new words had been coined and were current in the Christian community. The discoveries of papyri in Egypt were convincing proof that so-called "New Testament Greek" was just the ordinary language of home and business and government in the commercial towns around the Mediterranean in the first century.

In the Seminary there were some who were decidedly allergic to languages, but for the most part we accepted the acquisition of Hebrew and Greek as essential preparation for the ministry. Gesenius' *Hebrew and Chaldee Lexicon,* and Thayer's *Lexicon of New Testament Greek* were in every student's room. Complaints were offered by critics of theological education that so much concern with the original tongues left students unacquainted with the contents of the Bible; but in comparison with the student of twenty-five and fifty years later, the men of the '90's knew their Bibles.

The curriculum was Bible-centered, and almost Bible-bounded. In practical theology, Dr. Adolphus F. Schauffler of the New York City Mission Society taught Religious Education. He was a skilful artist on a blackboard. I can still see him writing a huge "B" upon it, and then placing "ible" opposite the upper loop of that letter, and subsequently "oy" opposite its lower loop, and telling us that our task was to get the Bible into the Boy. He possessed a singular gift for picturesque teaching and unquestionably had succeeded in making vivid to hundreds of children and adults the Scripture narratives. It was the era when Sunday School teachers and Christian parents had boys and girls memorize verses. Such memorization later became derided by religious educators; but as one who was its beneficiary, I should like to confess my unbounded gratitude to those who rendered so much of the Bible a lifelong possession.

During the 1890's the center of theological interest shifted from the Old to the New Testament. Debate arose over the composition of the Gospels and Acts, and over the authorship of the Epistles. It was at this point that Dr. McGiffert's *Apostolic Age* became the object of attack. Many who had freely used historical investigation in the narratives of Israel's history shrank from applying it to incidents in our Lord's career. Bishop Gore in England and Professor Briggs at Union were conspicuous instances of men who allowed the Apostles' Creed to set the boundaries of their critical probing.

Towards the end of the nineteenth century, scholars were examining religions among savage tribes and scrutinizing the cults which had contended with Christianity in the Graeco-Roman world. Frazer's *Golden Bough,* published in 1890, became widely read among students a decade later. When I began hearing sermons in the homiletic classroom in 1904 it was common to listen to the customs of primitive peoples or the myths of the first century as illustrations of Biblical passages. It is unlikely that they assisted in the conversion of sinners or the edification of saints.

Then, like a gust of fresh air blowing into a stuffy room, came Walter Rauschenbusch's *Christianity and the Social Crisis,* with its thesis that

The essential purpose of Christianity is to transform human society into the kingdom of God by regenerating all human relations and reconstituting them in accordance with the will of God.

Rauschenbusch had labored as a pastor in an underprivileged neighborhood in New York City, and he spoke with the passion of a prophet and the sympathy of a friend of the oppressed. Our students, many of whom were working in social settlements and in institutional churches and knew at first hand tenement-house conditions, heard in this fearless book the essential Gospel. They had listened to Jacob Riis speaking on *How the Other Half Lives,* and read in Lyman Abbott's *Outlook* similar writers on social conditions. It was the epoch when immigrants at the rate of one or two million a year were pouring into the country, and most of them through the Port of New York. The social conscience had been roused by Dr. Parkhurst, a Director of the Seminary, and by President Theodore Roosevelt. Rauschenbusch's book had an instantaneous effect. It displaced such side issues as comparative religion; words like *taboo* and *mana* lost their fascination for would-be preachers, and congregations were relieved. No longer did the minutiae of Biblical criticism delay the sermon on its way to a point. Social sins and social redemption by God's grace in Christ—here was the background in human need and here the Gospel. It was, from the point of view of a half century later, incredibly optimistic; but it was an evangel, and it fired those who proclaimed it. The teaching in Dr. Thomas Hall's classroom was reinforced; indeed it was outrun, and students complained that he did not analyze socialism and show its relation to the Gospel. This emphasis upon the salvation of society remained for the next three decades a dominant interest.

For ten years or longer, psychology had been a popular subject in many colleges. In 1902 William James had delivered his Gifford Lectures in Edinburgh on *The Varieties of Religious Experience,* and these were published and read with avidity. Professor George A. Coe at Northwestern had been working along this line, and his first two books, especially *The Religion of a Mature Mind* (a presumptuous title!) were winning a wide public. His election in 1909 to a Professorship at Union was hailed with enthusiasm. His courses were popular from the day he arrived, and his psychological teaching further stressed the social interpretation of the Christian message. At his coming his interests and those of his colleagues seemed to coincide. Later he attempted to cut the curriculum loose from its Bible-centered structure. He drew a sharp distinction between "transmissive" and "creative" education; but the Church which does not faithfully transmit her heritage is impotent to create full-statured Christians. This effort of his, vigorously pushed, brought him into conflict with President McGiffert and most of his colleagues.

An alumnus who studied at the Seminary in the second decade of the century, subsequently a leader in the life of the entire Church in this country and abroad, writes:

Religious education was coming to be the great new interest. Theology was regarded as rather an old-fashioned concern compared with the fresh and vital impulses that were expected from psychology and education.

The "social gospel" was just on the horizon, not yet a dominant emphasis. There were several students who were interested in settlement houses and the Labor Temple; but the chief concern was with the personal experience of the individual—particularly in the "reconciliation" of religion and the scientific view of life. Our proximity to John Dewey and some of his Columbia colleagues doubtless accentuated this.

The outbreak of the First World War in 1914 raised the

question of Christian Pacifism and divided the Seminary. The pacifist group was small but vocal. Some of its members were genuine pacifists, others pro-German. Professor Thomas C. Hall, with a delightful German wife whom he had married during his student days in Göttingen, espoused the German side. When the *Lusitania* was sunk, he defended the act in the press and on the platform. One of the Directors, Dr. L. Mason Clarke, resigned in protest in order to dissociate himself from the Seminary. The Board laid the resignation on the table, but Dr. Clarke refused any delay. President Francis Brown, also with a German wife, and with close friends on both sides in the European conflict, did his utmost to maintain harmony. Dr. Hall went to Germany in May to lecture and in the following autumn went to Switzerland where he worked with prisoners of war. In November 1916 he was granted by the Directors a further leave of absence, and Professor Harry F. Ward of Boston University was invited to take over his classes.

President Francis Brown died on October fifteenth and Professor McGiffert was appointed Acting President. In April the United States declared war and Professor Hall's status became a matter of discussion in both Faculty and Board. The Faculty had a frank expression of opinion, but took no action other than to express its confidence that the Acting President would convey their opinions to the Board. On May fifth the Board refused Professor Hall's request for further leave of absence, and voted

that, because in the judgment of the directors, Dr. Hall's attitude towards and his public expressions upon the moral issues in the war disqualify him from the occupation of the chair of Christian Ethics in the Seminary, therefore be it

Resolved that in view of the fact that we believe that the usefulness of the Rev. Thomas C. Hall, D.D., as a teacher in this Seminary has been destroyed, we hereby terminate the relation heretofore existing between Dr. Hall and the Seminary.

Meanwhile both members of the Faculty and students were going off on errands connected with the national service. On April thirtieth a public meeting was held in the Chapel at which President McGiffert, and Professors W. A. Brown, Coffin and Fosdick spoke. Dr. McGiffert said among other things:

This Seminary is an American institution, chartered by the State of New York, protected by its laws, deriving its liberties from the Constitution of the United States. It is a Christian institution, devoted to the progress of the kingdom of God at home and abroad; but it is also an American institution, and it owes its allegiance and loyalty not to God alone, but to country as well. So I want to take this opportunity to make public declaration of the loyalty of our Seminary to the country in this time of crisis, a loyalty symbolized by the flag that floats from our library tower. And I am sure I speak for our Board of Directors and for our Faculty as well when I say that if the Seminary can serve the country in any way, or by any special form of service, it is ready and eager to do so.

This statement was taken down and released to the press.

The decade which followed upon the Peace of Versailles was spiritually lean. Dr. McGiffert laid stress upon the Seminary as a theological university and disclaimed obligation for the vocations into which its students went at graduation. Its doors were open to all who desired its education. Many students with no dedication to the Church entered and took more courses in the University, particularly in Teachers College, than in the Seminary. Chapel services were slimly attended. Religious Education and Philosophy of Religion seemed the dominant interests. In 1922 Dr. Coe broke with the President over Dr. McGiffert's unwillingness to change the whole direction of the curriculum, and he accepted a post on the Faculty of Teachers College. Dr. McGiffert's health, never robust, began to fail and in 1925 he was voted a year's leave of absence and Professor William Adams Brown was made Acting President.

The Board sought the leadership of a minister with pastoral experience, and elected Henry Sloane Coffin, then pastor of the Madison Avenue Presbyterian Church. It laid upon him the task of changing the spiritual climate of the Seminary and developing it once more into a training school for servants of the Church. This involved a struggle—a struggle complicated later by public events and the sentiments of many students. Almost at once he was waited upon by a group of five who disagreed and disliked his initial statement to the alumni at Commencement. He had stressed the language of the Preamble the "claims of the world upon the Church." Four out of the five were preparing for careers outside the ministry of any of the churches. After listening to them, he informed them that since they were not purposing any ministry connected with the Church these four could not continue to occupy rooms in the dormitory. One student is said to have stood on the steps of the administration building in the quadrangle and to have announced loudly "Union Seminary will mark time until Henry Coffin is underground in Woodlawn."

But the spiritual climate changed swiftly. The Chapel

services were much more numerously attended. A course in the Minister's Message, by the President, taken the first year by only eight men became a staple for almost all seniors. Efforts were steadily put forth to bring the Seminary into close association with the Churches. With the dedication of the useful and beautiful small chapel off the lobby of the Refectory building, provided by his son in memory of the Rev. Lewis Lampman, D.D., of the Class of 1870 and Director from 1893–1918, students planned and carried on daily services, usually just before the evening meal, and sometimes again later just before retiring. These services, supplementing daily morning Chapel in the hands of the Faculty, helped to build a fellowship of worship, and gave students the chance to become familiar with the diverse traditions represented in the Seminary and to experiment in forms of their own devising. The value of these services varied with the taste, skill and spiritual quality of those who arranged and conducted them; but the contribution made by them to the Seminary cannot be overestimated. Students of music co-operated very enrichingly with students of theology.

With the coming of Reinhold Niebuhr in 1928 and of John Baillie in 1930 new intellectual currents began to flow. Perhaps the most significant trend in Protestantism was the emphasis upon the essential role of the Church. This became a potent factor in the thinking of the Seminary. The Church as organized in the churches had been viewed sociologically as one of several institutions ministering to the community; it had not been regarded as an object of Christian faith, and the body of Christ an essential element of the Gospel. There was a resurgence of belief in the Holy Catholic Church. The Church was seen over against the secular age with its science, commerce, patriotism, education, and so forth, resting on godless assumptions. Presuppositions in psychology, in ethics, in industrial relations were challenged. The current immanentism in philosophy was scrutinized and found defective in the light of the Christian Gospel. New interest in worship developed, happily reinforced by the School of Sacred Music. To be sure, the vast majority of music students pursued their work quietly; and the Seminary's life ran along with its emphases upon study and worship and practical work in the churches. The upheavals to be mentioned must not be taken as normal occurrences, but as unusual happenings, which reveal the current social life in the country and particularly in its universities, amid which the Seminary had to carry on.

But social radicalism continued rampant among many students. A society was formed named "The Agenda Club," whose professed aim was not inquiry or discussion, but action. The President spoke of it as "The Leap-before-you-look Club." Its members assumed that the underdog in any social conflict was always right. They picketed with strikers, even when they knew next to nothing of the issues at stake. A group of students wished the women who cared for the rooms in the dormitory dismissed and every student bid to make his own bed and keep his room clean. When it was suggested that this would involve a daily official inspection, the majority of the student body opposed it. Then the wages of Seminary employees were studied and plans for their increase advanced. The Board of Directors meanwhile had engaged a firm to make a survey of the situation, and as a result pay was materially augmented. But Soviet Russia was now claiming admiration, and a plan was put forward for a complete revision of the structure of the Seminary with employee and student representation upon the Board of Directors. An effort was made to have all the employees of the Seminary unionized. Most of the employees were hostile to the plan. One elderly woman who made beds and cleaned rooms was dealt with by the ardent reformers and told that her morals were middle-class. In a temper she came to the President and demanded a hearing before the Board to clear her name: "There's not a woman working in the dormitory, Mr. President, whose morals are not o.k." When assured that her and her colleagues' morals were those of the President and Professors, she was pacified. The Board happily had upon it several patient men who met with committees of upsurgent students and gave much time to listening to their generous impulses. But in the spring of 1935 some wilder spirits rose at night and ran a red flag up on the Seminary pole. The police appeared early in the morning to demand its removal and the raising of the Stars and Stripes with whatever other pennant might be flown.

The picketing by students carrying banners to the effect that "Union Theological Seminary protests the injustice, etc.," of the firm in question had brought a notice from the administration querying the right of students to represent the Seminary. At Commencement at the Alumni Luncheon the speaker for the outgoing class announced that a fascist despot now ruled the Seminary. The alumni fortunately took it humorously, and after some semi-facetious speeches the incident passed. In the Class of 1934 one of the graduates on leaving the Chapel is reported to have torn up his diploma. When no attention was paid to the rumor, he and a classmate appeared at the President's office, and asked for an interview. When asked why he had done this adolescent action, he replied that he wished to receive nothing from the capitalist system. When further asked how he would divorce the Seminary from that system and still keep it going, his replies were extremely vague. It was a pitiful exhibition of generous emotion devoid of mature thinking. Neither man has served a church. Their classmates happily regarded them as extremists.

During these years of occasional social agitation, there was a strong movement in our universities against War. Annually a student "Strike Against War" was called, and a demonstration held on the South Field at Columbia. Meanwhile the international situation became more ominous with Mussolini and Hitler rattling their sabres. These peace demonstrations were always set at an hour which conflicted with classroom exercises, and the students requested a holiday for their "strike." The President protested this annual interruption of Seminary work, but it was a principle with many members of the Faculty that student requests for "worthy ends" should be granted. The President's patience reached its limit in April 1936, and when the Faculty voted the desired holiday, he asked permission to have his written dissent entered upon the Minutes. It is as follows:

With grateful acknowledgment of the courtesy of my colleagues in allowing me to enter a dissent, although as presiding officer I had no vote, I desire to record my protest against the above action of the Faculty as an acquiescence in the attempt to introduce annually or oftener into the Seminary a form of coercion, compelling professors and students to interrupt the discharge of their academic obligations.

I am heartily in favor of Peace, and have spoken and stood for it at a time when it was much less popular than at present. I am also glad to share with students and professors in a collective demonstration against the iniquity and folly of War at any suitable time. But I protest on principle against allowing a group of students every year to set an hour for a demonstration which conflicts with classroom exercises and to exert pressure on faculty and students to abandon tasks to which they are obligated. Obviously it is possible to organize the demonstration at a time not pre-empted by academic exercises.

If this is a "student strike" (as I am informed it is labelled in the literature of its promoters) faculty cooperation should not be asked. A "strike" with the benevolent patronage of those "struck against" is a piece of infantilism unworthy of the intelligence of men considered fit candidates for the Christian ministry.

If this is not a "strike" but a demonstration for Peace in which the cooperation of faculties is desired, it would seem self-evident courtesy that representatives of university administrations should be asked to serve in choosing the date and hour and in making arrangements.

Inasmuch as those who initiated these demonstrations and have thus far engineered them apparently have deliberately planned them so that faculties, and in many instances students, should be coerced, this seems a vicious use of pressure, ostensibly in the noble cause of Peace.

If our students cannot detect and resist this pressure, how will they stand up under the fierce pressure of a war-inflamed patriotism? If a faculty does not resist such pressure, what becomes of academic freedom?

In my judgment the introduction into this Seminary of such coercive methods, with which I am happily confident most of our students do not sympathize, is calculated to injure the fellowship of Christian gentlemen, which has been and is our delightful heritage.

As one charged with maintaining the spirit of our Charter, I must enter my respectful protest.

When this statement had been signed and posted, Professors Bewer, Hume, Scott, Dickinson, Van Dusen, and Richardson requested permission to add their names to it. The statement had the desired result, and subsequent demonstrations were orderly meetings where the Christian attitude toward War and Peace was discussed from various points of view.

The students of that generation were the victims of a one-sided propaganda. At Student Christian conferences there were frequent speeches upon the sinfulness of participation in War, and it was assumed that the teaching of Jesus forbade such participation. There was no presentation of the complexity of international relations, whence wars arise; nor was anything said of loyalty to country as part of Christian duty. Pacifism, like Christian Science, was the refusal to employ approved means, and the substitution for them of love without further discussion of possible methods of using it both for the oppressed and their oppressors. An entire generation of young people, and particularly Christian young people, was totally unprepared for the realities of the world. The Fellowship of Reconciliation carried on a vigorous pacifist propaganda.

Professor Reinhold Niebuhr, who had been a member of this Fellowship, broke with it and set himself to inculcate a realistic Christian ethic devoid of sentimental absolutes. The presence on the Faculty of two victims of Hitler's ruthless persecution—Professors Tillich and Kroner—brought home to students the cruel facts of despotism. After the most bloody and brutal assaults upon the German Jews, an invitation was given to the Faculty and students of the neighboring Jewish Theological Seminary to share with us in a memorial to the victims. It was a moving occasion from which few went away unaffected. But there was an intransigent nucleus of pacifists who would not face such facts but fell back upon their interpretation of the teaching of Jesus that love, and love alone, was the obligation of Christians. It did not appear to penetrate their consciences that love for tyrants must show itself at the same time as love for their helpless victims.

When War broke out in 1939, Niebuhr and a group of like-minded associates founded *Christianity and Crisis,* and started on an educational campaign to alter the thinking of the American Churches. It was an effective sheet, read and quoted from extensively on both sides of the Atlantic, but the pacifist menace continued, and was strong in the student body at Union. When the Selective Service Act was passed by Congress in 1940, twenty students banded themselves together to refuse registration. Originally they hoped to align the entire student body with themselves, but they failed. They attempted methods of religious pressure—prayer meetings, and so forth—which went on during a large part of the night, and left those who joined in them mentally and physically exhausted. They publicized their position in the Press and over the radio and were joined by some divinity students and others in various institutions. The clamor throughout the nation was loud and bitter. Editors asked who in that Union Seminary Faculty had put the students up to this fatuous undertaking. Radio commentators had a field day. Cranks of

various types flocked to the Seminary to meet these heroic
young men and share, if possible, in their public acclaim or
obloquy. Their names were scarcely mentioned: they were
"twenty Union Seminary students" who proposed to defy the
law in the name of conscience.

The Selective Service Act had been carefully drawn to
provide exemption for conscientious objectors to War, and,
further at the instance of the Roman Catholic Church, it
exempted candidates for the ministry. The President of the
Seminary was in a peculiarly awkward position because the
leaders of the Fellowship of Reconciliation, when the law
was before Congress, had appealed to him to obtain a hearing for their representatives. He was personally intimate with
the Secretary of War, Henry L. Stimson, and at his request
Mr. Stimson arranged to have Dr. Fosdick and Bishop Apple-
ton Lawrence heard by the committee framing the Act. Now
it was in our Seminary that this scheme to flout the law had
erupted. It was entirely possible for these young men to be
legally exempted under either provision, but they desired to
combat the "war-system."

The situation was most trying. These students were sincere Christians and capable young men; one wished to protect them, even while they were bent on injuring themselves.
With such publicity, it was questionable whether any future
in the ministry would be possible for them. The name of the
Seminary was heralded not only in the metropolitan Press
but in every provincial newspaper, and the insinuation made
that its Faculty must harbor sinister characters. The Directors were daily importuned by friends and acquaintances to
clean out this nest of traitors and law-breakers. The Union
Seminary Board was a tried body and could not be stam-

peded, but the Auburn Board had just entered into partnership with us, and were even more troubled by this incident than their metropolitan confreres.

Not one of the students involved was a resident of New York City, so our first effort was to induce them to go to their homes for this act of civil disobedience where they could have the counsel of their parents. This they promptly declined to do. Accordingly, their parents were telegraphed and informed of the jeopardy in which their sons were placing themselves. In most instances there was a quick response, and some parents came on to New York. One, however, wired that his son was climbing the hill of Calvary and, were the Seminary President anything like as good a Christian, he would be climbing it with him. The Faculty was called to meet, and at once passed the following resolution which was given to the press:

The Faculty express their appreciation of the earnest attempt of these students to discover the course which they ought to pursue as Christian citizens in this confusing day. We recognize that there are circumstances when individuals or groups may deem it necessary to refuse to follow the will of government because to do so would be to deny their religious convictions. But in our judgment refusal to register in accordance with the Selective Service Act does not involve this principle. When the elected representatives of the nation enact a law which takes account of the rights of a minority, they conform to the traditions of democratic government. In this Selective Service Act provision is made for conscientious objectors to participation in military training and an opportunity is afforded for such objectors to state their views. To refuse to register and supply the government with factual information is to refuse what any government has a right to ask of its citizens. No member of the faculty has advised any student to follow this course of action.

This was adopted with practical unanimity. This Faculty action set them right with the public as widespread editorial comment the next day disclosed.

Then a special meeting of the Directors was called. Their officers had been kept informed and had counselled the President almost daily. When the proposal was made to dismiss these students summarily, it was pointed out that they were not breaking Seminary rules but proposing to defy the law of the land and that the Government could and would deal with them; and further that their expulsion might, indeed probably would, add to their number fellow-students who were sympathetic and would deem them harshly treated. The Board understood the student situation and took no action.

Meanwhile constant personal interviews were taking place with the students and messages were received daily, sometimes at midnight or after from their anxious parents. Twelve of the twenty decided to register. The judge of the court before whom the eight law-breakers would appear sent his clerk to see the President of the Faculty, and ascertain what he thought a fitting sentence. He assured him that the men would appear at the registry, and therefore would not be "draft-dodgers." He urged that their statement against registration be received as evidence, and that the judge should point out in court their folly, rebuke them as severely as he thought wise, and let them off. It still appears that this course would have robbed them of "martyrdom" and been an expedient action for the government. It would have given their sympathizers no ground for complaint or compassion. But the judge thought that since the Act called for training for at least a year, they should be sent to jail for that time. Their sympathizers still visited them, and were somewhat of a nuisance. The wrath of the administration blazed at leaders of the Fellowship of Reconciliation who had importuned the President to help them the previous summer, and now encouraged these younger men in their hazardous course. One maiden lady who came daily to cheer them, had indited a poem and brought it to the President's office with the request that it be read to them. It ran somewhat as follows:

> O ye heroic, steadfast eight,
> To God and duty dedicate,

and went on at length in this monotonous meter. The President's secretary sent for the eight, but after the opening lines had been heard, one of the victims expressed preference for prison to the suffering of listening to this poem. In pity the reader desisted but pointed out the character of the support they had enlisted.

It was a tense day in the Seminary when these eight went off to be sentenced. The President and Comptroller went down to visit them in the detention prison, where the warden of the federal penitentiary at Danbury who was to receive them had already talked with them and had an accurate judgment of who were ring-leaders and who followers. The President saw him later after he had had them in the penitentiary where they had protested prison regulations, particularly the segregation of colored prisoners in the mess-hall, and had been frankly told that they were not there to reform the prison but to be themselves corrected. The warden remarked, on bidding the President good-bye: "Sir, I thought that as warden of a penitentiary I had difficult men to deal with; but after my acquaintance with these chaps, I hand it to you." Here again was the *obstinatio,* of which Roman officials complained in first century Christians.

When the Auburn Directors held their next meeting, several of them objected to the weakness with which we had handled this incident. They saw every reason for prompt expulsion of such students, and asked whether we thought jail-birds should be allowed to go on into the ministry. The President recalled to them St. Peter, St. Paul and St. John on Patmos. This came apparently as a startling surprise, and nothing further was said on the subject.

After this heart-breaking incident, the Seminary settled down to its regular work. The effect of the refusal to register was to make other students more determined to do their full part in the fighting forces, and one of the most brilliant, waiving exemption as a theological candidate, had a notable career in the army as an officer, and was reported missing after the bitter fighting in the Battle of the Bulge. One morning at Chapel he was eulogized by a professor, as though dead. This was premature and, happily, assurance came of his safety. The harrowing events of the War sobered the student body, and radical agitation ceased. Student interest became centered upon systematic theology. Men felt that a desperately needy and sinful age must have an affirmative message of salvation. This emphasis appears to continue. Certainly it should be the dominant concern of a theological college. A younger member of the Faculty writes:

Twenty years ago the main problem was one of getting students to relate their social hopes sufficiently to a foundation in the Gospel. Today the main problem is one of helping them to see how the Gospel, to which they are already thoroughly committed, can lift them, not merely in "idea" but in heart and soul out of the despair in which they find themselves and their world.

While the students of two decades ago were vocal in suggesting remedies for all the world's ills, and covered bulletin boards with petitions to the President of the United States or Congress or some other public authority, those of the present generation feel too confused to prescribe for mankind. They have recently been spoken of as "the silent generation"—that is evidence of their hesitancy and of their intense preoccupation with the complex questions life forces home upon them. It is a much more favorable atmosphere for profitable theological study.

# CHAPTER XI

# THE LIBRARIES

IT is an evidence of the lofty scholarly hopes of the founders that as early as 1838, in the midst of their struggling days of poverty, they set about the organization and development of a theological library. Its nucleus, collected by a former Benedictine monk, Brother Leander Van Ess, was termed at the time of its purchase and importation "the most valuable library that has ever been brought into this country." This initial collection had an interesting history. It was part of the library of the Monastery of St. Mary at Paderborn, where it constituted the *libri prohibiti* under the charge of Brother Leander. In 1801, when the Peace of Lunéville threatened the sequestration of the property of religious houses, the Benedictines of Paderborn divided their possessions among themselves and removed to places of greater safety. Van Ess went to Marburg, where he became Professor in the Roman Catholic Faculty. Later he collaborated with Protestants, notably the British Bible Society, in translating the Bible into the vernacular languages. Whether or not he himself embraced Protestantism seems uncertain. When the Union Directors learned that the Van Ess collection might be secured, they appropriated $5,070.00 for its purchase, although it was necessary to mortgage the Seminary's property to raise this sum, and faculty salaries were badly in arrears.

Three foremost scholars in succession had charge of Union's theological library—Professors Edward Robinson, Henry B. Smith, and Charles A. Briggs—with the result that in its growth it included the outstanding books of the middle years of the nineteenth century in the various fields of theology, and was enriched by the personal libraries of Professors and alumni. On June 30, 1953, it totalled 249,513 volumes, 97,523 pamphlets, and 3,097 manuscripts and typescripts—probably the most extensive theological library in the English-speaking world.

Among its treasures are large holdings of incunabula ("cradle books" which antedate 1500), and Bibles, Greek Testaments and Gospels from the five hundred years which have passed since the invention of printing. The chief strength of the library lies in the historical field, where many and most of the definitive editions of the Church Fathers, both Western and Oriental, are available. There is an almost complete Zwingli collection, a thousand items in or about Luther, and three hundred items connected with John Calvin. The McAlpin collection of British history and theology, collected by Professors Briggs and Dr. Ezra H. Gillett and his son, Dr. Charles R. Gillett (librarian 1883–1908), aided by the munificence of the late David Hunter McAlpin (director 1872– 1901) is surpassed in completeness only by the British Museum and the Bodleian at Oxford. It contains some 17,000 books and tracts printed before 1701, relating to the religious movements of the stormy seventeenth century; and a collection of the books and pamphlets on the Deistic and Trinitarian controversies of the eighteenth century is a worthy sequel. There are also many histories of Great Britain, both local and general, her churches, universities and the biographies of leaders in her religious life.

In more recent years a library of religious and moral education has been opened in a separate room to which many publishers have contributed their books. With the establishment of the School of Sacred Music, another room was set apart where the Samuel A. Baldwin collection of organ music and Emma Thompson Shuman collection of piano music are housed along with such valuable sets as *Analecta Hymnica Medii Aevi, Tudor Music,* Zahn's six massive volumes on the tunes of the Evangelical Churches of Germany, and Bäumker's volumes on German Roman Catholic music. The Newman collection of more than 1,400 volumes, the property of the Hymn Society of America, is also kept in this room.

The late Professor William Adams Brown had an extensive library on systematic theology and allied subjects which at his death passed to the Seminary, and is now available as a special collection for students in these fields. He was also an enthusiast for, and diligent worker in, the ecumenical movement, and the William Adams Brown Ecumenical Library, a collection on the World Church set up in his memory and embracing Dr. Brown's private papers, is the official depository for the World Council of Churches and the fullest collection of research materials in this field in the Western Hemisphere.

Immediately after the World Missionary Conference at Edinburgh in 1910, under the leadership of Dr. John R. Mott, the missionary boards of the Protestant Communions began to assemble a Missionary Research Library containing more than 70,000 books and pamphlets. The Seminary had honored the memory of President Charles Cuthbert Hall by assembling a collection on missions, on the cultures and religions with which these have to deal, and on the younger churches. In 1929 the leaders of the Missionary Research Library came to the Seminary seeking space in which to house under fireproof conditions their valuable possession. With the assistance of one of the Seminary's directors, Arthur Curtiss James, the Brown Memorial Tower was fitted up to contain the offices and stacks of this Library and the Charles Cuthbert Hall collection was combined with it, making a total of some 82,000 volumes—probably the greatest missionary library in the country, if not in the Protestant world. Its first curator was the late Charles H. Fahs. This Library is operated and financed by a joint committee on which the Mission Boards place eight representatives and the Seminary four. It is the first such co-operative enterprise in which the Seminary is associated with the official agencies of most of the Protestant Communions. Its present director is the Rev. Dr. R. Pierce Beaver, formerly a missionary in China. It renders a valuable service not only to the various Boards located in New York, but also to the many missionaries on furlough who do further study in the city, and to many who come here purposely to avail themselves of its information.

In the Seminary libraries is a large body of material upon the religious history of the United States. The Gillett Fund, named in honor of the Rev. Ezra H. Gillett, the David Dudley Field and other collections of pamphlets, have covered the various controversies in the religious thought of this nation. The reports of ecclesiastical bodies, many histories of the various Communions and of individual congregations, the minutes of official conventions, assemblies, and so forth, a carefully made selection of books on American history, on political and social thought in this nation, a wide range of biographies of leaders, together with surveys of church and community, and works of many varieties on social welfare, supplement this material and make the collection most valuable for students engaged in research in any field of American Church life.

The Seminary had several catalogues for its various library collections, and these were not uniform. In 1909 Miss Julia Pettee came on the staff, and introduced order into the relative confusion, conforming classifications to those of the Library of Congress. She remained until 1938 when she had completed the catalogue for almost the entire Library. This makes every book or pamphlet easily accessible.

When Auburn entered into partnership with Union in 1939 her library of some 12,000 volumes was combined with that of the Seminary, enriching it in many fields.

# CHAPTER XII

# THE SEMINARY
# AND WORLD SERVICE

FROM its outset, Union Seminary had focussed its eyes
upon the entire globe as belonging to Christ and to be made
His to its uttermost parts. In the statement adopted in the
house of Knowles Taylor on Bond Street the founders spoke
of "the claims of the world upon the Church of Christ"; and
these claims were constantly before its students. Many men
of eminence went out under various Church boards into both
home and foreign missionary fields. In its first century ending 1936, one out of twelve of its alumni had gone to the
foreign field.

From the half dozen members of its second class (1838)
Samuel Robbins Brown took ship for the one hundred and
twenty-five day voyage to China, where, since women were
not admitted, his young wife entered listed as "freight."
Brown brought the first Chinese to America for study. In
1843 Henry Martyn Scudder went to India under the American Board and settled in Madras. After eight years he asked
for an area less occupied by Christian enterprises and became a founder of the Arcot Mission of the Reformed Dutch
Church. The Arcot Mission is now part of the Church of
South India. The Scudder family is conspicuous in missionary

annals and is estimated to have given over a thousand years to active service at home and abroad.

The class of 1847 contained a man of unique powers and intense spiritual experience, George Bowen, whose fascinating biography was written by Robert E. Speer. Bowen was the son of a wealthy New York merchant, a self-made man who did not believe in education and put his boy to work. After a few years the young Bowen determined to educate himself, which he did largely in public libraries, and equipped with German, French, Spanish and Italian, he travelled extensively in Europe becoming the correspondent of the papers of that epoch in New York. Returning to the United States, he entered on a literary career in which he attained distinction and was admitted to the Knickerbocker set—a coterie gathered about Washington Irving. An avowed unbeliever, his articles showed a strong anti-Christian bias. But the death of his loved fiancée brought on a spiritual crisis. In a complete about-face he soon entered the Seminary and threw himself into Christian work in the city. He was aflame with devout enthusiasm and kindled his fellow-students, many of whom like him turned their eyes towards missions as their career. Leading student prayer-meetings, he began those deeper experiences of the life of the Spirit which were later to issue in profound devotional articles which gave him a world-wide audience. On graduation he at once sailed for India, and toiled with untiring energy for forty years without furlough or change of climate. With no evident results from his efforts, he flung himself more entirely upon God and refused to be discouraged. His fellow-missionaries persuaded him to employ his brilliant literary gifts, and he became editor of the *Bombay Guardian*, which soon attained a circulation far beyond India numbering among its readers Queen Victoria and Henry Drummond, who attributes part of his spiritual biography to Bowen. Bowen had but one ambition: so to conform his life to his Master's that in him Christ might walk the streets of Bombay as He had those of Jerusalem. He gave up his missionary salary in order to live on the level of the coolies about him; he occupied a bare room in a mud-walled house; he spent his days preaching in the streets and bazaars and his nights often in prayer; he frequently fasted for long stretches. His passionate love of Christ and resolve to follow Him without compromise has seldom been rivalled. Enormously ambitious, as his confidential diary attests, in his old age he wrote to a sister in Fordham: "I told the Lord this morning that I was content to be everlastingly insignificant" —a unique Christian whom God employed to infect others with his glowing devotion, but in ways usually hidden from Bowen's eyes and other than he himself intended.

From the Class of 1855, Henry Harris Jessup sailed for Syria with seven other missionaries on a vessel laden with New England rum. He formed his missionary purpose early in his Seminary course, attended medical lectures and studied dentistry, and worked as a distributor of tracts on Blackwell's Island, at the Five Points Mission, and the Half-Orphan Asylum. Just before sailing, he returned to the Seminary for a missionary prayer-meeting where he knelt with Harding, later of India, White of Asia Minor, Byington of Bulgaria and Kalopothakes of Athens. The next day he preached in Newark suggesting to the young people that they write after careful thought—"Resolved, that if the Lord will give me grace, I will become a missionary." Among those who followed his plea was a small boy, James S. Dennis, whose later writings in Arabic became classics, and who has left the Church the three weighty volumes: *Christian Missions and Social Progress.* Jessup spent fifty-three eventful years in a constantly confused Near East, and left an impress on educational institutions and the Christian movement in that fanatically Muslim area of the world.

In the Class of 1852, John Thomas Gulick became a missionary to Japan, where his career is conspicuous for independent thinking. A biologist, as well as a theologian, he was an early advocate of the theory of evolution and applied it in his work. He was scrupulous not to transfer his pattern of American Christianity to Japanese minds, but encouraged them to arrive at their Christian convictions and ideals through their own best thinking—a man whose methods were true to those of his theological *Alma Mater.*

From the Class of 1870 went "Characteristic" Smith, so-called from a book he wrote on *Chinese Characteristics,* which became a best-seller. With irrepressible wit, much prized by the Chinese as well as by his numerous American listeners and readers, he labored for fifty-four years. A Christian statesman, he recommended to President Theodore Roosevelt that the Boxer indemnity should be returned to China and applied to Chinese education, a course which Great Britain also followed.

From the Class of 1871, John Henry House went out to Bulgaria. Living through the Russo-Turkish conflict, he helped in the exchange of prisoners. He became Director of the American College and Theological Institute in Samokov, Bulgaria, 1874 to 1891. Then in 1894 he founded the Thessalonica Agricultural and Industrial Institute, the fulfilment of his dream that in this agricultural land young people should be trained to be leaders in the lines along which the population must labor. The Greek Government appreciated his efforts, and his Institute has turned out boys efficient in many practical skills. He introduced the American wild grape-vine, grafting delicious Greek grapes on this stock which resisted successfully the plant lice at that time infesting the vineyards and threatening them with ruin. He showed himself fearless in his trips through bandit-filled mountains, where among other achievements he rescued the captured Miss Ellen M. Stone. He died in 1936 at Salonica in his ninety-first year.

From the Class of 1882, Gilbert Reid pursued a unique career in China. He went out under the Presbyterian Board but resigned from it in 1894 that he might not bring criticism upon it by his unusual methods. A broad basis of scholarship and a fervent personal faith enabled him with courage to approach representatives of other faiths. He founded the International Institute of China, an approach to the educated classes. It attempted to establish a better understanding between folk of all religions. The platform on which he based this enterprise was too broad for most Christians and Reid plowed a solitary furrow until his death in 1927. His career was a marked instance of courage, vision and selflessness.

From the Class of 1886, Sidney L. Gulick, born of missionary parents in the Marshall Islands, spent twenty-six fruitful years under the American Board in Japan, and then twenty years in this country in the service of the Federal Council of Churches promoting international justice and good-will. It was a time of increasing tension between the United States and Japan, and Dr. Gulick rendered valuable service in attempting to lessen it. It was he who thought up the quota system of immigration on a basis proportional to the nationals already here, and finally got the Exclusion Act of 1924 repealed. He sponsored various Friendship projects, by which Doll Messengers of Friendship went to Japan, School Bags were sent to Mexico, Friendship Treasure Chests were filled for the children of the Philippine Islands, and Friendship Folios were forwarded to China. A number of valuable books and pamphlets came from his mind and hand, which helped to sweeten and Christianize international relations.

From the Class of 1887, Howard S. Bliss, the son of the pioneer missionary in Syria, Daniel Bliss, went out to assist his father. The latter had established at Beirout the Syrian Protestant College, later known as the American University, an institution which drew students from all over the Muslim world. Howard Bliss had been a brilliant student and received the travelling fellowship in his class which he used for study at Oxford, Göttingen and Berlin. On his father's death, he became President of the University and it fell to him to pilot it through the stormy years of World War I and the scarcely less perilous years which followed. His courage and tact were extraordinary. Amid the cross-currents of that turbulent area, with strife and starvation all about him, in imminent peril of deportation from suspicious German or Turkish officials, he won the respect and affection of even his enemies. He pled for Syria before the representatives of the Allies in Paris met to frame the Treaty of Peace, basing his argument on his trust in the people and in their capacity to work out their political salvation. When he died, former students from every Muslim center sent tributes, and men of every faith praised the services of one whom they regarded as among the great of their generation.

In the Class of 1896, Horace Tracy Pitkin was the leader in the missionary meetings of his day. He had committed himself to the cause at the Northfield Student Conference when he was a freshman at Yale. Under his contagious influence a missionary revival took place both at Yale and at the Seminary. While still studying for the ministry, he travelled from college to college as Secretary of the Student Volunteer Movement, and under his leadership at least one hundred students volunteered who actually reached the field. Among those who felt the effect of the Spirit in Pitkin's life was George Sherwood Eddy. The two classmates knelt in Pitkin's room in the Seminary, praying that God's plan for Eddy's life should be made known, and Sherwood Eddy became a flaming evangelist all over the world and a force for Christ for the rest of his long life. Pitkin went out to China on graduation, but had scarcely learned the language and started work at Paoting-fu when the Boxer uprising darkened the horizon. The station was cut off, but the brave company waited in serene trust in God, whatever might be their lot. Pitkin wrote: "We must sit still, do our work and take quietly whatever is sent." The fanatical Boxers arrived, and on July 1, 1900, Pitkin was beheaded while attempting to shield two women missionaries. A tablet to this missionary martyr adorns the wall of the cloister by the Chapel and is passed by hundreds of students every day.

Oliver H. Bronson, also of the Class of 1896, ministered with Yale-in-China at Changsha, and again at Peking for a brief space. Edwin O. Lobenstine and DuBois S. Morris, 1898, with James B. Cochran, 1896, established the outstanding station at Hwai Yuen in Anwhei, and Lobenstine later for twenty years was the Executive Secretary of the China Council of Churches.

The more recent classes of the twentieth century have sent out their graduates to the foreign field. Herbert S. Harris, 1900, spent eight years in Cuba, and later more years at Rio de Janeiro. From 1903 Edward S. Cobb taught for a liftime in the Doshisha in Kyoto. His classmate, Alden H. Clark, spent fourteen years as Principal of the Marathi Union Training School at Ahmednagar, returning in 1918 for a short period to the office of the American Board in Boston, then becoming Principal of the United Theological College at Ahmednagar until 1929, when he was chosen Secretary of the American Board. From this same class of 1903, Brownell Gage was provost of Yale-in-China for twenty years, and W. H. Gleysteen was an outstanding missionary in Peking for more than forty years. The Class of 1904 gave Robert Ernest Hume to be Professor at the Seminary at Ahmednagar and Editor of a Christian weekly in Bombay, and Daniel J. Fleming to be Professor in Forman Christian College in Lahore; both returned to occupy posts on the Union Seminary Faculty. 1906 sent out Charles H. Corbett for eighteen years to China, Robert Simkin for over forty years in the Friends' Mission in the same land, and Charles L. Boynton to serve in the Y. M. C. A. and the American School in Shanghai. 1907's brilliant scholar, Murray S. Frame, went to the school at Tungchow and died at Tientsin in 1918; James McC. Henry spent years as President of the Canton Christian College (Lingnan University); and Edmund DeL. Lucas headed the Forman Christian College in the Punjab. From 1908, Robert B. Elmore went out to devote his entire lifetime to work in Santiago, Chile, while Artley B. Parson after a few years in Manila returned to become a Secretary of the Protestant Episcopal Board, and Lucius C. Porter dedicated his

life to teaching in Yenching University at Peking. From the
Class of 1909, George A. Fitch served the Y. M. C. A. in
China and received various honors from the Government—
the "Order of Brilliant Jade," among others—and on FRGS
from Great Britain, and A. C. Salley devoted arduous years
to Brazil mostly at Sao Paolo in MacKenzie College and as
executive of the Central Brazil Mission of the Presbyterian
Board. Thomas C. Carter, 1910, started the flourishing mission at Nanhsuchow, Anwhei, China, where he was joined by
George C. Hood, 1911, who continued there for a quarter
of a century while Carter returned to take the Chair of
Chinese at Columbia University. John Stuart Burgess, 1910,
served at the Princeton University Center in Peking for fifteen years. For ten years he was Professor and Chairman of
the Department of Sociology at Yenching University in Peking. Charles A. Carriel, 1911, was for a number of years in
educational institutions in Brazil and his classmate, Reuben
H. Markham, became a conspicuous figure in the Balkans
under the Y. M. C. A. and as journalist. Another classmate,
Cass A. Reed, became Principal of the International College
at Smyrna and for a brief while a Professor in the American
University at Beirout. Still another from this Class of 1911,
Frank Slack, after serving in India and Ceylon under the
Y. M. C. A., headed the Foreign Division of the International
Committee. The Class of 1912 had Herbert A. Boyd of the
Canadian Presbyterian Church serving under its Board in
China, S. Ralph Harlow and William R. Leete under the
American Board in Smyrna and in China respectively, and
Luther Fowle in Turkey. The Class of 1913 had Bayard
Dodge at Beirout where he succeeded Howard Bliss as Presi-
dent of the American University and carried it through the

vicissitudes of the Second World War with enhanced prestige; Frank C. Laubach as a missionary in the Philippines who developed a method of overcoming illiteracy and became an international figure spreading his system in many lands; John R. Lyons, who spent some years at Shuntefu in Northern China; and James Thayer Addison who after a period at St. John's College in Shanghai returned to take the Chair of Missions in the Episcopal Theological School in Cambridge and to serve in the Episcopal Board of Missions; another part-time member of the class, Charles A. Stanley, served in China and was for a time Dean of the Cheloo School of Theology at Tsinan in Shantung. The Class of 1914 made a notable contribution to the missionary cause in five of its men—W. B. Albertson who served under his Canadian Methodist Church in China until his death in 1940; Ross A. Hadley, who, after a short service in India, became Secretary of the Friends' Board for Missions; Harold C. Jaquith, who invested himself in the Near East in Greece and Turkey; Theodore D. Walser, serving under the Board of the Reformed Church in Japan; and William P. Roberts who became Bishop in the Protestant Episcopal Church in Shanghai. In the Class of 1915, Marion E. Hall worked for years in Japan under the Y. M. C. A. and the American Board, ending there as Professor for seven years in the Doshisha; Laurens Seelye who taught philosophy in the American University at Beirout and at Robert College in Istanbul; John B. Griffing served in Nanking University and later as Director of an Agricultural College in Brazil; and Lawrence Mead served under the Y. M. C. A. at Nanking and Hangchow, again in the Princeton-in-Peking center for eight years and finally on the Faculty of Yenching University. From 1916, Stanley A. Hunter taught for a period in Ewing Christian College at Allahabad. From 1917, Homer H. Dubs was in China and became a Professor in Chinese at various institutions and finally at Oxford University; Henry Smith Leiper went out as a missionary to China under the American Board and returned later to become an Associate General Secretary of the World Council; Herman Carl Steinheimer worked in China and in Puerto Rico in educational work. From 1918, Carl Bare was pastor in San Juan, Puerto Rico, and in Calcutta, ministering to churches for English-speaking congregations; Philip Allen Swartz worked in China and in Hawaii for nine years; Fred Tredweld Smith served under the Y. M. C. A. in the Near East and taught in the American University at Beirout and at Cairo; and Elmer T. Thompson, after spending five years as a missionary in Japan, returned to become Candidate Secretary of the Baptist Foreign Missionary Society and later Director of the International House in Philadelphia. In the Class of 1921 Egbert Hayes interrupted his seminary course to become Educational Secretary of the Y. M. C. A. in Shanghai, and later filled posts in Nanchang, Soochow and Peking; Wendell M. Thomas became a missionary of the Friends in India; and William P. Woodard served under the American Board in Japan until the World War compelled his withdrawal in 1941. In the Class of 1929 Victor Neal Maricle, after serving in various Y. M. C. A. posts in this country, went to Chile, where he is head of the Y. M. C. A. in Santiago and a prominent factor in the evangelical missionary community.

From the 1920's on, one notes a marked difference in the record of the Classes. In the campaign for funds conducted at the close of World War I a number of missionary fellowships and scholarships were provided for, and the new building on Claremont Avenue contained apartments for missionaries on furlough. A choice group of them availed themselves of these openings and studied with us, adding much to the Seminary's life. Their more mature spiritual experiences and intellectual gains contributed to the classes which they attended. Many of them were conspicuous figures in the missionary force, and they came from all over the face of the earth.

In the first fifty years of the Seminary's history, Professor Fleming found only two nationals from the foreign field enrolled in the student body. This changed markedly in the next half century, when students in numbers came from various fields. From 1924 the Student Friendship Fund, raised by Union Seminary Faculty and students, was awarded anually to an outstanding national from one of the Younger Churches, (a misnomer in some instances for the Orthodox Churches of South India are among the oldest in Christendom). It has been Union's distinction to aid in the preparation of a number of the most influential leaders in the Churches of Asia, South America, Africa, and the Pacific Islands, including:

Timothy Tingfang Lew, '18, Professor and Dean of the School of Religion in Yenching University, Peiping, China. Member of the Legislative Yuan of the National Government of China.

William Hung, '20, formerly on the Faculty of Yenching University in China, and now on the Faculty of Harvard University, Director of the Harvard-Yenching Sinological Institute.

Yu-Yue Tsu, '21, Bishop in the Anglican Church in China, formerly Professor in St. John's University, Shanghai.

The Rev. Andrew Thakar Dass, '24, for thirty-three years pastor of the Naulahka Church in Lahore, largest Protestant congregation in Pakistan, Moderator of the United Church in Northern India, 1936–38, chairman of the Trustees of Forman Christian College, and Executive Secretary of the National Christian Council of West Pakistan.

Tetsutaro Ariga, '24, Professor of Christianity at the National University in Kyoto, able leader of the Japanese Church, Henry W. Luce Visiting Professor at Union Seminary, 1953–54.

Pao-chien Hsü, '24, Professor in History and Philosophy of Religion, Yenching University, Peiping, China, until his death in 1944.

Shakir Khilil Nassar, '27, teacher in various schools and colleges, principal of the Boy's School, Tripoli, Lebanon, translator of a number of Dr. Fosdick's books, working in the American Legation at Beirout on Point Four Program.

Rajah Bhushanam Manikam, '28, formerly Executive Secretary of the National Christian Council of India, and the First Joint Secretary of the International Missionary Council and the World Council of Churches for East Asia.

The Rt. Rev. Johannan Mar Timotheus, '30, (formerly Cherukara Matthew John), Metropolitan of the Mar Thoma Syrian Church in Travancore, India.

Alfred J. Ferreira, '31, Principal of the Carlton van Heerden High School, at Upington, South Africa.

George Benjamin Molefe, '39, Principal of the Newell African High School, New Brighton, and the first African Moderator of a Presbytery in South Africa.

David G. Moses, '33, Principal, Hislop College, Nagpur, India.

Wallace Chun-Hsien Wang, '40, first Chinese President of the West China Union Theological Seminary in Chengtu, China.

Takashi Murakami, '40, Professor of Systematic Theology at the Doshisha University, Kyoto, who met an heroic death in a Russian prison camp after World War II was over. In the same institution: Setsuji Otsuka, '15, Dean of the Department of Literature, 1916–1947; The Rev. Sadao Yamada, '20, Professor of History; The Rev. Tadakazu Uwoki, Professor of Church History, 1927–52; Sumio Ogata, '54, Professor of Systematic Theology.

Benjamin Ignacio Guansing, '41, President-elect of the Union Theological Seminary, Manila, Philippine Islands.

Terenig Vartabed Poladian, '41, formerly President of the Armenian Theological Seminary Antelias, Beirut, Lebanon, now Bishop of the Armenian Church (Catholicos).

Surjit Singh, '45, on the Faculty of the Theological Seminary at Saharanpur, India, more recently teaching at San Francisco Theological Seminary.

Alexander Rotti, '48, serving the Y. M. C. A. in Indonesia, and influential member of the Indonesian legislature.

Kunnumpurath Mathew Simon, '48, Executive Director of the Third World Youth Conference at Travancore 1952, and Bishop-elect of the Old Syrian Orthodox Church.

Malieckel George Chandy, '49, Bishop of the Mar Thoma Syrian Church of South India.

Joshua Russell Chandran, '50, President-elect of the United Theological College, Bangalore, India.

Harold S. Hong, '52, Acting President of the Methodist Seminary at Pusan, Korea.

Among former European fellows who are distinguished leaders of their churches may be mentioned the following:

Joseph Krenek, '08, Moderator of the Evangelical Church of the Czech Brethren.

H. Emil Brunner, '20, for many years Professor of Theology at Zürich, also at Princeton Theological Seminary, now on the Faculty of the Japanese International Christian University, one of the most influential contemporary theologians.

William Cumming Thom, '21, formerly President of the Faculty of Theology at Sydney, Australia.

The Rev. Sir George F. McLeod, '22, has held important charges in the Church of Scotland, St. Cuthbert's Edinburgh, Govan in Glasgow, and is the founder of the Iona Community.

Philippe Henri Menoud, '30, Professor of the New Testament at Neuchatel, Switzerland, who held a similar post at Lausanne, 1934–46.

Dietrich Bonhoeffer, '31, Professor in the "underground" theological faculty in Germany during World War II, executed by the Nazis at Dachau just before the U. S. A. troops arrived. Gisevius in *To The Bitter End* gives the story of this heroic resistance to Hitler.

Arnold L. Mobbs, '33, pastor of the Reformed Church at Celigney, Switzerland, and Secretary for Ecumenical Matters of the Swiss Reformed Church.

Vassil Georgieff Ziapkoff, '34, Pastor of the First Evangelical Church in Sofia, victim of the Communist persecution, whose "confession" according to Dr. J. Hutchison Cockburn was patently the result either of torture or of drugs.[1] Imprisoned for ten years.

Happily also a number of the Faculty travelled on missionary errands and were familiar with Churches in other lands. Dr. Charles Cuthbert Hall had twice been Barrows Lecturer in the Far East. George William Knox had been a

---

[1] *Religious Freedom in Eastern Europe*. Richmond, Va.: John Knox Press, 1952. Ch. 4.

missionary in Japan and a well-known figure in the Imperial University at Tokyo; he died in Seoul while serving as Union Seminary lecturer on Christianity to the Far East. Professor William Adams Brown served on the same lectureship in 1916; and again in 1930–31 he was one of a commission to assess Christian Higher Education in India. Professor Frame lectured at the Doshisha in 1906 and in 1920 spent the summer in China, Korea, and Japan. Professor Coffin spoke at the Kuling Convention in 1916 and was also in Korea and Japan; Professor Fosdick had a similar appointment in 1921. Professor Elliott was in China as the Secretary of Bishop Bashford in 1905–8, studied for the Methodist Church the problems of administration in Japan and China, inaugurated the China Centenary Campaign, 1908–10, and assisted Bishop C. Hartzell in the Africa Diamond Jubilee Campaign. Professor Erdman Harris taught in the American University in Cairo, 1925–28. Professor Hume, born of a noted missionary heritage in India, had been on the staff of the theological school at Ahmednagar, and in 1923 lectured on India's Early Religious History at the Universities of Bombay and of the Punjab. Professor D. J. Fleming had been on the Faculty of the Forman Christian College at Lahore, 1904–12, was on the Commission on Village Education in 1919 and one of the fact-finders for the Laymen's Foreign Missions Inquiry in 1931. Under the auspices of the National Christian Councils of India and China, Professor Ward had lectured in those lands. Professor and Mrs. Lyman, Professors Bewer, Scott and Tryon lectured in the Near East. Professor Arthur Jeffery was a missionary in India and a Professor in the School of Oriental Studies at the American University in Cairo at the time of his call to Columbia and Union. Professor Walter S.

Davison served as Chaplain at Robert College in Istanbul, 1927–30. Professor Iglehart who succeeded Dr. Fleming had spent 1909–42 in Japan and Professor Searle Bates had been Vice-President of the University of Nanking when he took up his work at Union in 1950. President Emeritus Coffin filled the Joseph Cook Lectureship under the Presbyterian Foreign Board in 1946–47, and Dr. George A. Buttrick lectured on the same foundation in 1951. President Van Dusen has twice circled the globe in the interest of the Christian World Mission, visiting various countries of Asia and Africa, and attended the Conferences at Tambaram and Lucknow. His work in the Ecumenical Movement has brought him in close association with the Church leaders of the Younger Churches. Professor John C. Bennett rendered outstanding service as a Lecturer in India and Japan, where ministers and theological students in the Churches discussed their problems with him, and his book on *Christianity and Communism* has been widely read and used. Beginning in 1951, a special program of study on this theme has been given at the Seminary each year under the auspices of the Foreign Boards, where many missionaries were present; the group was presided over by Charles W. Forman, 1944, of the United Theological College in Saharanpur. In all the centers of the Churches in Asia, Europe and Africa a member of Union's Faculty is met by groups of graduates, both nationals and missionaries, grateful and loyal to their theological *alma mater*. At our daily prayers in the James Chapel we face our Lord's command: "Go ye into all the world," and the words carry our minds over the earth and link us with a vast company of fellow alumni in our thought and prayer.

# CHAPTER XIII

# THE SEMINARY AND THE
# ECUMENICAL MOVEMENT

DEEP in the hearts of the founders of Union Seminary
and of those who have led and taught in it throughout the
years was the passionate desire for the ending of denominational divisions in the Church of Christ and the unifying of
all her people for the achievement of the ends set before
her by her divine Head. The Seminary's Professors and Directors have been foremost in the work of interdenominational organizations.

Professor Briggs' Graduate Chair bore the title of "Ency-
clopaedics and Symbolics"; and under the latter head he
dwelt on Irenics—the science and art of seeking reconciliation among divided brethren and finding the underlying unity
beneath confessional differences. In his old age he sought
an interview with the Pope, and at some length explained
to Cardinal Gasparri a plan for the reorganization of the
Roman Curia in an effort to render it more palatable to those
on the outside and more in line with Biblical principles.
While this serious attempt betrayed Dr. Briggs' lack of
humor, it evidences the sincere purpose of this great Christian.

When in the twentieth century the Federal Council of
the Churches of Christ was set up, several of the Seminary's

alumni were among the leading figures who planned it. Samuel McCrea Cavert, 1915, became its General Secretary in 1920 and by wise tact developed it for the next three decades and made it a guiding force among the Churches. With him in its leadership were F. Ernest Johnson, 1912, Henry Smith Leiper, 1917, and Roswell P. Barnes, while Professor William Adams Brown toiled valiantly in soliciting funds for its support, and particularly for new outreaches of its efforts. Professors Coffin, Niebuhr, Van Dusen, Bennett, Roberts, and Richardson served also on its Executive Committee or on various subcommittees.

In November 1950 the National Council of the Churches was inaugurated at Cleveland, Ohio. Dr. Cavert, 1915, was the obvious choice for its first General Secretary. The details of its organization were largely the work of the statesmanlike mind of Hermann N. Morse, 1911, Secretary of the Presbyterian Board of National Missions, whose great abilities were recognized by his own communion in 1952 with a unanimous nomination and election to the Moderatorship of its General Assembly.

Two even more comprehensive movements of an international character had got under way—the Faith and Order Conferences originated in the Protestant Episcopal Church, and the Life and Work Movement due to the initiative of Archbishop Söderblom of Sweden. In these movements Dr. William Adams Brown was a very enthusiastic and helpful factor. He served on the Executive Committee of the Faith and Order Conferences and was indefatigable in seeking funds for their support. He was also a member of the Universal Christian Council for Life and Work, and one of the Presidents of its Conference on Church, State and Society at

Oxford in 1937, when the University of Oxford recognized him with other leaders of that assembly by conferring upon him the Honorary D.D. for his services in promoting the unity of the Church of Christ. Dr. Brown is appropriately remembered in the Ecumenical Library at the Seminary.

At this Conference in 1937 Union Seminary men were in conspicuous positions. President Coffin was Chairman of one of its sections which dealt with Church, State and Society in Education. Professor Van Dusen was a member of the section which dealt with Church and Community, and Professors Niebuhr, Bennett and Tillich of the section that handled Church, State and Society in Economics. Once enlisted in these ecumenical movements, these scholars could not demit responsibility.

At the first Assembly of the World Council of Churches at Amsterdam in 1948, President Van Dusen headed the committee which prepared the program in the area of the Church's message, and became Chairman of the World Council's Study Committee. Professors Bennett and Niebuhr were assigned posts which kept them, with Dr. Van Dusen, shuttling across oceans to attend meetings of committees. Professor David E. Roberts prepared materials for the Study Committee and lectured at the Institute in Bossey. Several alumni were connected with the World Council executive office; Dr. Clarence E. Josephson, 1932, was Associate Director of its Reconstruction Department, and was succeeded by the Rev. Robert L. Tobias, 1945; the Rev. Charles W. Arbuthnot, 1938, and the Rev. Charles C. West, 1945, (formerly missionary in China) became members of the staff of the Presbyterian Foreign Board in Europe, and associated with the World Council's reconstruction activity; the Rev. Paul R. Abrecht,

1946, became Associate Director of the Study Department. President Van Dusen calculated that at Amsterdam there were eighty-seven among the speakers, delegates, alternates, consultants and members of the Staff, who had been teachers at or held degrees from Union Seminary.

In 1947 St. Vladimir's Seminary of the Russian Orthodox Church, which had been leading a somewhat vagrant existence, was offered the use of classrooms, chapel, library, and dormitory space at Union. The invitation was accepted. The Dean, the Very Rev. George Florovsky, has been made an Adjunct Professor of Union where he was preceded by an expert and learned layman, the late George Fedotov. Dr. Florovsky is also a teacher in the Department of Religion at Columbia University, where he offers three courses. The students come from the several groups who in this country make up the constituency of the Orthodox Church. There were forty-one of them in 1951. They must be eligible for the undergraduate department of Columbia when they enroll in St. Vladimir's.

It is a distinct gain to Union to have this contact with the Christian East, now so sorely oppressed under Communism, and contact with Union students, as well as those of Columbia, assists the students of St. Vladimir's to understand American thought and life, and so be prepared to minister in their churches in this country. The place which the Orthodox Churches of the East now fills both in the National Council of the Churches in the United States and in the World Council of Churches renders it vital that they should be understood by and should more clearly understand the other Churches with whom they are affiliated. Too long Eastern Orthodoxy has lived to itself in isolation from the West, and too long the West has viewed Eastern Orthodoxy as a quaint survival of an outworn past, rather than as a living factor for Christ in the present.

The inclusion of St. Vladimir's Seminary among the components of theological education on Morningside Heights seems a direct answer to a prayer of Professor Philip Schaff. When he was being inaugurated at Union in 1872 he remarked, speaking of the varieties of Christianity in the United States:

Only the Eastern or Greek Church, the oldest of all, has as yet scarcely a name in the young western world.

Dr. Schaff believed profoundly that God had brought representatives of all the Churches to live side by side in this country that we might become familiar with one another:

This co-existence and social commingling of the different phases of Christianity, each representing a peculiar set of ideas and a correspondent mission, must facilitate a thorough acquaintance, remove many prejudices, and foster a spirit of large-hearted Christian liberality and charity. . . . In our land, if anywhere on God's earth, is a field for actualizing the idea of Christian union, which shall gather into one the best elements from all ages and branches of Christ's kingdom.

Union is no dead uniformity. . . . The Church of God on earth is a spiritual house with many stories, and each story has many apartments; to be in this house at all, we must occupy a particular room, which we are bound to keep in order and adorn with the flowers of Christian graces. But what should hinder us to live on the best terms of courtesy and friendship with our neighbors and brethren who occupy different apartments in the same temple of God, who love and worship the same Christ, who pray and labor as earnestly as we for the glory of our common Master and the salvation of souls, and with whom we expect to spend an endless eternity in the many mansions of heaven?[1]

How Dr. Schaff would rejoice, could he see the Christians of the Eastern Church moving about with the Union students of our day in the same halls and presenting to the world this symbol of oneness in their sharing of a training for the one Christian ministry!

## ECUMENICAL SCHOLARSHIP

There have been other ecumenical enterprises, in the sense that they crossed denominational boundaries and were shared by Christian scholars of many Communions, in which the Seminary has borne a part.

The first is the revision of the Bible, bringing its translation to date both in respect of the text used where subsequent generations had become possessed of manuscripts or versions or had acquired new knowledge which enabled them to handle the Hebrew and Greek originals more accurately, and in respect of the changes in a living language so constantly expanding in extent and altering in shades of meaning as is our English tongue. When in the 1870's it was resolved to proceed with a revision of the King James translation, an American Committee was organized to co-operate with a similar committee in Great Britain, and Professor Philip Schaff was elected its President. This American Committee continued in existence after the Revised Version was published in its British form in the 1880's, and the American Revised Version appeared in 1901.

---

[1] *The Theology for Our Age and Country,* Rogers and Sherwood, 1872, pp. 81 and 22.

Under the auspices first of the International Council of Religious Education, and later of the National Council of the Churches of Christ in the U. S. A., a new revision was resolved on. Dean Luther Weigle of the Yale Divinity School was chairman of the Committee of Revisers, and our Professor James Moffatt was invited to serve as Executive Secretary of the Committee which had the New Testament in hand, while Professors W. Russell Bowie and Frederick C. Grant were also members of this Committee. Their Revised Standard Version of the Bible appeared on September 30, 1952. As the earlier committee under the presidency of Dr. Schaff had met frequently at the Seminary buildings of that epoch, so the New Testament Committee of the RSV had often come together in Professor Moffatt's office.

In four other undertakings of ecumenical scholarship, Professors and graduates of Union have shared to the enrichment of the Church. The first was the publication of *The International Theological Library* of which Professor Briggs was an editor together with Principal Stewart D. F. Salmond of Aberdeen. In this monumental enterprise George Foot Moore, '77, contributed the two massive volumes on the *History of Religion,* Dr. Arthur Cushman McGiffert wrote the *History of Christianity in the Apostolic Age,* Dr. James Moffatt wrote the *Introduction to the Literature of the New Testament,* Professor Henry Preserved Smith was the author of the volume on *Old Testament History,* and Professor Charles A. Briggs was advertised as preparing two volumes on *Theological Encyclopaedia* and *Christian Symbolics,* but died before these were completed. President Francis Brown was assigned the volume on *Contemporary History of the Old Testament,* when his election to the Presidency of the Seminary interrupted his scholarly labors and proved so absorbing in time and strength that he was unable to fulfil this assignment. Professor William Adams Brown's name also appeared on the list of prospective authors for the volume on *The Doctrine of the Christian Life*, but this book, too, was never written.

Parallel with this *International Theological Library*, the *International Critical Commentary* was projected, of which Professor Briggs was also an Editor in conjunction with Professor S. R. Driver of Oxford and the Rev. Alfred Plummer, D.D., Master of University College, Durham. In this commentary *Judges* was the work of George Foot Moore, '77; *Samuel* of Professor Henry Preserved Smith; *Chronicles* of Professor Edward L. Curtis, '79; the *Psalms* of Professor C. A. Briggs. In the two volumes on the *Minor Prophets*, Professor Julius A. Bewer wrote those on *Obadiah, Joel*, and *Jonah*. Dr. Francis Brown's assignment, *Kings*, never came from his pen for the reason given above on his projected history. In the volumes of the New Testament, Professor Marvin R. Vincent prepared the volume on *Philippians* and *Philemon*, Professor James E. Frame the volume on *Thessalonians*, and Professor James Moffatt the volume on *Hebrews*.

A half centry later another commentary was projected— *The Interpreter's Bible;* it was clearly stated that it was not to be another critical commentary, but was intended for ministers "on Main Street." It was laid out to do for them what the *International Critical Commentary* and the *Expositor's Bible* had together attempted—an accurate exegesis and introduction and an exposition for practical life. It is planned for twelve large volumes, containing introductory articles of fine scholarship but plainly and untechnically written, and every book of the Bible is put in the hands of an exegete, a technically competent Biblical scholar, and a preacher with an eye for the relevant in a passage and an understanding of the needs of human souls. In this undertaking Union Seminary is cast for a great role. Its Editor, George A. Buttrick, is on our Faculty, as are the four Associate Editors; for exegesis, John Knox and Samuel L. Terrien respectively are professors in the New Testament and in the Old Testament in our classrooms, while the two Associate Editors for exposition, W. Russell Bowie and Paul Scherer, are Professors in the Seminary's Department of Practical Theology. As one's eye runs over the contributors to these bulky tomes, Union Seminary names are everywhere; thirty-two or just one-fourth of the writers are drawn from the Faculty and alumni. Under *Ecclesiastes* the expositor, Gaius Glenn Atkins, is a Professor Emeritus of Auburn; under *Ephesians* and *Colossians,* Francis W. Beare was a graduate student and a lecturer on New Testament Greek in 1944–45; under *Genesis* the expositor is our Dr. Bowie, '08, as of *Luke* chapters 1–6, and he is also the writer of a delightful article on "The Parables." Dr. Buttrick is the expositor of *Matthew* and author of the article on "The Study of the Bible." Albert G. Butzer, '20, writes the exposition of *Numbers,* James T. Cleland, '28, contributes the expositions of *Ruth, Nahum* and *Zechariah,* 9–14. Phillips P. Elliott, '25, performs a similar task for *Judges;* Charles W. Gilkey, '08, for *Ezra* and *Nehemiah;* S. MacLean Gilmour, '28, furnishes the introduction and exegesis of *Luke,* Professor Frederick C. Grant, the introduction and exegesis of *Mark;* his son, Robert M. Grant, '41, contributes the general article on *The Ancient Period* in "The History of the Interpretation of the Bible." William H. P. Hatch, the unique holder of a D.D. conferred in '15, is the writer of a general article in "The History of the Early Church," dealing with *The Life of St. Paul.* Paul W. Hoon, '34, is the expositor of *I, II, and III John.* Professor Arthur Jeffery supplies two general articles on "The Canon of the Old Testament," and on its "Text and Ancient Versions," besides writing the introduction and exegesis of *Daniel.* Professor John Knox supplies the exegesis of *Romans* and the exposition of *Luke 7–12,* Halford E. Luccock, '09, has given us the exposition of *Mark,* Sidney Lovett, '18, the same for *Amos.* Professor John T. McNeill writes on the *Medieval and Reformation Period* in "The History of the Interpretation of the Bible." William P. Merrill, '90, is the expositor of *Lamentations,* Morgan P. Noyes, '20, of *I* and *II Timothy* and *Titus.* James Muilenburg contributes the general article on *The History of the Religion of Israel,* and the introduction and exegesis of *Isaiah 40–66* of which President Emeritus Coffin, '00, is the expositor. Harold C. Phillips is expositor for *Hosea;* Professor Scherer furnishes expositions of *Job* and of *Luke 19–24;* Rolland W. Schloerb, '20, is the expositor of *Proverbs.* John C. Schroeder, '21, contributes the exposition of *Samuel,* Professor Ernest F. Scott writes a general article on *The Beginnings* in "The History of the Early Church" and the introduction and exegesis of *Philippians;* Ralph W. Sockman, '16, is the expositor of *I Kings,* Theodore C. Speers, '25, of *Zechariah 1–8;* Samuel L. Terrien, '36, writes the general article on *The Modern Period* in "The History of the Interpretation of the Bible," and the introduction and exegesis of *Job.* Robert R. Wicks, '08, contributes the exposition of *Philippians.*

One looks with satisfaction at this weighty contribution to a commentary designed to assist preachers. The Seminary has surely not neglected the study of the Scriptures.

Finally, mention may be made of the new Library of Christian Classics, in which Union Seminary is playing an important role. The series is being edited under the joint supervision of President Henry P. Van Dusen, '24, Professor Emeritus John T. McNeill and Principal John Baillie of Edinburgh, formerly of the Union Faculty. The first volume, *Early Christian Fathers,* by Professor Cyril C. Richardson, '32, has appeared and Professor Wilhelm Pauck is preparing the translation of Luther's *Commentary on Romans.* A completely new translation of Calvin's *Institutes,* with introduction and annotations, is being prepared by Dr. McNeill as the copestone of this noteworthy addition to theological scholarship.

# AFTERWORD

## UNION SEMINARY: 1945–1954

### BY HENRY P. VAN DUSEN

Although Dr. Coffin has, at a number of points, carried this history beyond 1945, for the most part he has concluded his narrative, as was intended, with his retirement from the Presidency of the Faculty. Some not inconsiderable changes have occurred in the life and program of Union Seminary in the past nine years. A brief summary of the more important developments may serve to give a picture of the Seminary as it faces toward the future.

## THE STUDENT BODY

The alumnus of a half-century or even a quarter-century ago who returns to Union today is likely to be struck, first of all, by the marked increase in *enrollment*. While the Seminary had never established a fixed figure as the ideal size for its student body, the average annual enrollment through the two decades between the World Wars had been less than 250 regular students, and the largest (in 1930) had been 314.[1] In each of the nine years since the War, the corres-

---

[1] In addition, there are always 100 to 200 students registered for a few courses. They are disregarded here. The Summer Session which annually enrolls about 400 and the July Ministers' Conferences which enroll over 300 are also excluded.

ponding figure has not been less than 500, twice the pre-War average.

This influx was foreshadowed in the final year of Dr. Coffin's Presidency when, as the conflict drew toward its close, veterans began to turn toward the ministry in unprecedented numbers. For some time, it was assumed that the increase would be temporary. But, as year followed year, no noteworthy diminution occurred. The figure continues at about 550. Nor is there any indication that the flood-tide will soon ebb. On the contrary, the source-springs of supply in the colleges and universities appear to be overflowing. More important than numbers, however, is quality of applicants. Here, likewise, these latter years have witnessed a heartening improvement. This is a hopeful day for the oncoming leadership of the Christian Church.

Not less interesting is the composition of the Seminary student body of today. It consists of four fairly distinct groups of students, pursuing parallel programs of study leading to different degrees.

At the heart of the Seminary's program, making a first claim upon its resources and upon the concern of every member of the Faculty, are the candidates for the degree of Bachelor of Divinity, most of them in direct preparation for the pastoral ministry of their several denominations.

Of late years, a report has become current that Union Seminary is turning away from the training of men for the pastorate to give its major attention to post-graduate students. No impression could more directly contradict the facts. While the proportion of candidates for advanced degrees within the total student body is somewhat higher, the number of students in the standard program for the B.D. degree has been larger in every year since the War than in any year before the War, averaging between 225 and 250. This figure would be even larger were it not for a policy of rigorous limitation in enrollment. In the view of our Faculty, a theological seminary, like a medical school, can give the requisite training to only a certain number of students in any one class. The maximum figure has been fixed at 80 for each class, or no more than 250 for all B.D. candidates.

Not only is the Seminary preparing more men for the pastorate; more graduates are actually entering the regular ministry each year than ever before in Union's history. Indeed, nothing has been more characteristic of the post-War generation of theological students than their firm determination to give themselves to the "typical ministry," preferably at the grass-roots. One of them, an alumnus with distinction from one of the large Eastern universities who was directed toward the ministry during his wartime service in Army intelligence, was much sought after on his graduation from Union for teaching and chaplaincy posts in schools and colleges. He declined a number of attractive opportunities in order to seek out a typical small-town church in a typical middle-western community. This was his explanation:

I think of the local church as a "line company" of riflemen. This is the fighting, the cutting edge of the Army. All other service troops in the rear are necessary but they exist only to strengthen the "front." That's where Christians live and die and that's where we want to be, at least as long as we are of any use.

If the 225–250 B.D. candidates be thought of as occupying the central position in Union's program, they are flanked

on either side by groups of students preparing for specialized ministries supplementary to the pastorate. One is the
Ministry of Sacred Music. Between 75 and 100 men and
women are in training to become choir directors, organists
and teachers in this field as candidates for either the Master's or the Doctor's degree in Sacred Music.

Flanking the B.D. students on the other side, so-to-say,
are some 75 to 100 men and women majoring in religious
education with the intention of becoming directors of church
schools, church workers, leaders in student religious organizations, etc. In recent years, two alternative programs have
been offered, leading to the degree of Master of Arts in
Christian Education or in Religious Education, in collaboration respectively with Columbia University or with Teachers
College. In 1953, Teachers College, having for some years
no longer maintained a teaching staff in religious education,
decided to discontinue its Master's degree in this field. In
consequence, the Seminary is assuming full repsonsibility for
this program which has previously been maintained jointly
with Teachers College. Approval has been obtained from the
Regents of the University of the State of New York to add to
the Seminary degrees that of Master of Religious Education,
and a two-year course leading to that degree is being projected. There is special appropriateness in this development
in view of the fact that Auburn Theological Seminary prior
to the merger of its work with Union in 1939 conducted a
School of Religious Education leading to a Master's degree.

The fourth category in the Seminary student body embraces candidates for advanced degrees in theology or religion. Prior to the Second World War, students in this classi-
fication averaged about 50. Today, they number approxi-

mately 125. They are pursuing a variety of academic programs, leading to different degrees, as follows:

*Master of Sacred Theology.*

*Doctor of Theology,* the highest degree offered by Union Seminary. Heretofore, only advanced students in Bible, Church History and Theology have been eligible for the doctorate. Beginning with the academic year 1954–55, the Th.D. program is being broadened to open the degree to candidates in all phases of Practical Theology, including Religious Education.

*Master of Arts in Christian Education, in the Literature of Religion or Comparative Religion* at Columbia University.

*Master of Arts in Religion* at Columbia University.

*Doctor of Philosophy in Religion* at Columbia University. This degree, administered by a Joint Committee whose membership is drawn equally from the Faculties of the University and the Seminary, offers doctoral programs in four alternative fields—the History of Religion, the Literature of Religion, the Philosophy of Religion, and Religion and Society. Instituted in 1943, it quickly established itself as one of the most attractive and highly regarded doctorates in religion in the country, and a large number of the Seminary's increased enrollment of post-graduate students is to be found here.

*Doctor of Education* at Teachers College.


## FOREIGN STUDENTS

No single feature of the post-War period is more noteworthy than the accelerating increase in graduate students from abroad. Dr. Coffin has mentioned that, in the first fifty years of Union Seminary's history, foreign students numbered only two. In each of the past five years, the Seminary has welcomed between 60 and 70 foreign students from twenty to thirty different countries, about one-eighth of the total student body. In recent years, a number of individual congregations have made themselves responsible for the support of foreign students. The church contributes the amount of a fellowship and the recipient becomes the guest of the donor congregation during his time of study in the United States. The holder of the fellowship thus has the privilege of intimate hospitality within the homes and church life of a particular community, while the donor congregation is introduced to the life and work of the Christian World Movement abroad through some of its ablest young leaders, with mutually enriching results.

Virtually all of the holders of foreign fellowships are persons of maturity who have had not only basic theological education in their own lands but also a number of years of practical experience which have demonstrated their exceptional promise for future leadership. Increasingly, they are men or women who have already been selected for particular positions of importance, either in Christian education or in church life; they are sent to Union for quite specific training for their life tasks. It may be questioned whether any one phase of the Seminary's total program is making a more important contribution to the world-wide Church of Christ of tomorrow.

## FACULTY AND ADMINISTRATION

One of Dr. Coffin's most pointed and oft-repeated injunctions to his Faculty has been quoted earlier: "Union Seminary lives by its brains." His charge to his successor in the Presidency included this admonition: "Keep your eyes vigilant to detect theological luminaries rising on any horizon," but "make sure that these rising luminaries whom you espy are steady lights, and not mere flashes."

The ceaseless quest for scholarly talent continues a relentless duty as well as an exciting preoccupation. While the questions of the most desirable ratios between older and younger teachers, and between those trained at Union and those brought in from other schools, have never been matters of formal decision, practice has, in fact, answered them along rather definite lines. In contrast to some schools which depend almost entirely upon filling vacancies with younger men at junior ranks, Union Seminary has called to its Faculty in recent years an unusually large number of mature scholars already established in the leadership of their fields. The result is that the present Union Faculty is, relatively, heavily weighted at the top. It is surprising to discover, in a theological teaching staff of 36, no fewer than 23 at the rank of full professor. The present "Senior Faculty" is almost equally divided between men who have had their preparation and all or most of their teaching experience at Union and those whose training and early teaching experience has been elsewhere. Meantime, a group of younger scholars at junior ranks is being formed to supplement and relieve the Senior Faculty.

Since June 1945, the following additions to the Senior Faculty have been made:

> Lewis Joseph Sherrill
> Mary Ely Lyman
> Miner Searle Bates

George Florovsky
Wilhelm Pauck
Paul Waitman Hoon
Daniel David Williams

and the following have been elevated to the rank of full professor:

Arthur Lessner Swift
Hugh Porter
Richard Jacob Kroner
Cyril Charles Richardson
Frank Wilbur Herriott
David Everett Roberts
Samuel Lucien Terrien

Two newly endowed professorships, each unique in character, have added variety and strength to the Faculty. Mention has been made of the Henry W. Luce Visiting Professorship of World Christianity, created in memory of a member of the class of 1895 who had rendered distinguished service to Christian higher education in China. This Chair brings to the Seminary each year an outstanding scholar from one of the Younger Church areas who takes his place as a full professor on the Union Faculty, assumes a modest teaching responsibility and also has much free time for his own scholarly pursuits or service to the churches. Six Luce Professors from as many areas of the world have thus far held this appointment:

Francis Cho Min Wei, China
Paul David Devanandan, India
Lootfy Levonian, Lebanon

Gonzalez Baez-Camargo, Mexico
Zachariah Keodirelang Matthews, South Africa
Tetsutaro Ariga, U. T. S. '24, Japan

In 1953, Mr. John D. Rockefeller III presented the Seminary with an endowment to create the Harry Emerson Fosdick Visiting Professorship. Appointments to this Chair will also be for a single year and the appointees may be drawn from any part of the world, from laity as well as clergy, and from any religious affiliation. A unique feature of the gift is its stipulation that the Fosdick Professor will ordinarily spend half of the year of his appointment at Union and the other half in service to other theological institutions and churches throughout the country. The first Harry Emerson Fosdick Visiting Professor, Dr. (Sir) George Fielden McLeod, U. T. S. 1922, founder and director of the Iona Community in Scotland, is expected to take up his responsibilities in the autumn of 1954.

In 1950 Mr. Randolph H. Dyer was appointed to succeed Mr. Charles T. White and became Comptroller and Treasurer. In 1952 Dr. Edwin O. Kennedy, U. T. S. 1924, was appointed to the newly created office of Secretary of the Seminary.

## PLANT AND EQUIPMENT

Inevitably, physical facilities designed originally for a community of less than 300 have been severely taxed to take care of almost twice that number.

In the matter of student residences, through the hospitality of the James Foundation, the top floors of their building at Park Avenue and 69th Street (the Seminary's location prior to the occupancy of its present site on Morningside Heights in 1910) have been made available for women students to supplement the women's dormitory in McGiffert Hall. In Hastings Hall, the commodious single study-bedroom suites which formerly housed most men students are a thing of the past. The lower three floors of Hastings are now occupied by married couples. On the floors above, which are still reserved for unmarried men, single rooms have become doubles, and double rooms are now triples. In 1946, the Seminary acquired the apartment dwelling, Reed House, at the northeast corner of Broadway and 121st Street, directly across Broadway from Hastings Hall. Stringent rent-control laws have prevented occupancy of more than a few apartments. In them, however, the Seminary has been able to offer hospitality to its sister-institution, St. Vladimir's Russian Orthodox Seminary and Academy, and to a number of organizations such as *The Interpreter's Bible* and *Christianity and Crisis,* which are unofficially but closely related to the Seminary through the participation of Union Faculty members in their direction.

To provide enlarged academic facilities for the increased enrollment and developing program, two major and several minor reconstructions and additions to the existing plant have gone far to meet the need. In 1950, the terrace which previously flanked the Henry Sloane Coffin Administration Building at the southern end of the Seminary quadrangle was blasted out and, in the considerable space thus made available, the Mills Memorial Audio-visual Center, the gift of the Davella Mills Foundation, was constructed—a unit of classrooms, studios, control-rooms, and offices, all sound-conditioned and provided with equipment of the highest quality for the newer techniques in the use of films, radio, recordings, etc. Then, above the terrace level, Auburn Hall, a four-story building containing lecture and seminar rooms, academic administrative offices, a center for alumni activities and the Alumni Lending Library, and the headquarters of Auburn Seminary, was erected by Auburn Theological Seminary in recognition of ten years of happy and fruitful association with Union Seminary.

In 1953, donations from the James Foundation made possible provision of new and long-needed facilities for students of the School of Sacred Music. The interior of the tower above the James Memorial Chapel, which had been left in an unfinished condition, was completely reconstructed and sound-conditioned to house a classroom, a library, a Director's studio, and sixteen individual practice rooms, half for pianos and half for organs, the latter supplied with new or rebuilt instruments. Thus, the Faculty and students of the School of Sacred Music who had, a few years earlier, been characterized by a committee of Directors as "musical martyrs" struggling with inadequate instruments scattered in the "catacombs of the Seminary basements" are now blessed with superbly designed and equipped work-rooms.

Lesser remodelling has modernized and improved faculty apartments, married students' quarters and dormitories.

## FINANCES

If the contrast between the Seminary of the pre-War and post-War periods which most impresses the alumnus or casual visitor is the change in the size and diversification of the student community, a contrast which is an even more pressing reality to the administration is the altered situation in the Seminary's finances.

It has been widely supposed that Union Seminary is a wealthy institution, exempt from the fiscal worries which hound most educators. It is true that the generosity of a number of men and women of large means had provided it over the years not only with a superb physical plant but also with endowment of about $9,000,000, more than twice that available to any other theological school in the United States. Income on this endowment, supplemented to a minor degree by modest tuition fees (Union was the first seminary to charge tuition) and receipts from other sources, normally made possible a balanced budget. For the most part, the officers of the Seminary were free from day-by-day concern for the Seminary's solvency, and relieved of the necessity to organize support for current expenses or to solicit additional endowment, except for occasional special efforts, such as a major fund drive in 1924 to overcome the deficits accumulated during the First World War.

Radically new conditions in the post-War years have changed all that. Through new and strenuous measures to secure annual support to supplement endowment income, a deficit was avoided in each year up to 1952–53; but only by careful husbanding of resources, by rigorous economies, by placing a far larger responsibility upon the students themselves for the cost of their education, and, most important of all, by the enlistment of contributions to current expenses from a steadily enlarging number of alumni, churches, foundations and friends. To accomplish the latter necessity, a public relations program and staff was organized, and what had been no more than a periodic concern to previous Seminary presidents became an almost daily first-claim upon time and effort.

Finances are most clearly revealed in figures. The following comparisons over a decade tell the story of Union's drastically altered finances:

In 1943–4, the Seminary budget totalled $484,062; in 1953–4, $1,039,222.[1]

In 1943–4, income from endowment of $7,614,310 was $328,441 and accounted for 68 per cent of the budget; in 1953–4, income on endowment of $8,995,253 amounted to $440,000, but that was only 42 per cent of the budget.

In 1943–4, income from fees charged 261 students totalled $84,746, or 17 per cent of the budget and $324 per student. In 1953–4, with a student body numbering 572, the income from student fees totalled $258,400, or 25 per cent of the budget, an average of $452 per student.

In 1943–4, receipts from contributions accounted for only $42,983, or 9 per cent of the budget, and the number contributing was approximately 250. In 1953–4, the list of contributors had increased to more than 2,000, and their donations totalling approximately $188,350 represented 18 per cent of the budget.

During the decade from 1944 to 1954, the capital resources of the Seminary have been augmented as follows:

| | |
|---|---:|
| Gifts for Buildings and Plant | $ 696,370 |
| Additions to Endowment | 1,254,109 |
| | $1,950,479 |

---

[1] In these figures, certain self-sustaining services such as the Refectory and Book Store are omitted. Although their totals fluctuate somewhat from year to year, income roughly equals expenses. Therefore, they do not materially affect the Seminary's position.

## THE "STUDENT MIND"

From time to time, I have attempted to characterize the mentality of the typical Seminary student of today.

We are now dealing with the post-World War II generation. The first thing to be said about them is that the contrast between the generations which came to maturity before and after World War II is far greater than was the case with the pre- and post-World War I generations. They enter the Seminary, mature in experience and schooled in intimate familiarity with the world of this global Atomic Age. They are men and women most of whom have come of age and had all their higher educaton since the War. They present a quite distinctive mentality.

This is a generation doggedly in earnest but without solemnity; intellectually alert and eager; as quick in laughter as sharp in criticism; tenacious for every illumination of mind or quickening of spirit, with a disdain of all pomposity or sham or pretence; almost wholly free of the superficiality, the cynicism, the "smart-aleckism," the clerical professionalism which are the bane of youthful theologues; moved by a strong devotion without trace of sentimentality, and poignantly eager to be possessed by a Faith adequate to a day whose tragic and testing demands they understand so well. Their interest focuses upon the central theological issues. Their preaching will be marked by an austerity and an authority not often noticeable in their immediate predecessors, but well familiar to those who study the Gospel in its ages of greatest power. God as they discern Him and as they yearn to present Him convincingly to men is portrayed more in His majesty than in His nearness, more in judgment than in compassion, more as Sovereign Justice than as Everlasting Mercy. Above all, they are impatient with anything less than Christian Faith in its full richness, profundity, certitude.

# INDEX